MW00988434

Re-Script
YOUR FUTURE

POWER-PACKED PROCLAMATIONS FOR YOUR
LIFE, BUSINESS AND GOVERNMENT

Dr. Clarice Fluitt

Re-Script Your Future

Power-Packed Proclamations for
Your Life, Business, and Government

Re-Script Your Future

© 2019 Clarice Fluitt

All rights reserved. This book is protected by the copyright laws of the United States of America. This book may not be reproduced in any form, stored in a retrieval system, or transmitted in any form by any means; electronic, mechanical, photocopy, recording, scanning, or otherwise; without prior written permission of the author except as provided by United States of America copyright law.

Unless otherwise noted, Scripture quotations are from the King James Version of the Bible (Public Domain). Scripture quotation marked (NKJV) taken from the New King James Version®. Copyright © 1982 by Thomas Nelson, Inc. Used by permission. All rights reserved.

ISBN: 9781094882260

Publisher: Clarice Fluitt Enterprises, LLC

P O Box 15111. Monroe, LA 71207

claricefluitt.com

Endorsements

Among all the qualities I look for in a teacher, of utmost importance is the quality of intuition. Time and again Dr. Clarice Fluitt has demonstrated this ability with me personally. She has a unique ability to see the finished blueprint of a person's life while accurately reading the next step they need to take. When you find yourself getting stuck in the tunnel of transition of where you've been you can't go back to; and where you want to go you can't get there yet, use this book as your mile marker out and let the standard of attainment move your bar to a whole new level. Transition is powerful because it changes you, and this book takes you on the journey between two points where your spirit and your heart get wrapped around an entirely new reality. Find yourself as you turn the pages going from the mediocre middle of the mountain all the way to the top where your clear endings become your new beginnings.

As you continue moving toward your own life quest, I wholeheartedly endorse Dr. Clarice and her book

Re-Script Your Future: Power-Packed Proclamations for Your Life, Business and Government.

DR. LANCE WALLNAU
LANCE WALLNAU MINISTRIES
SPEAKER, LEADERSHIP COACH, BUSINESS CONSULTANT,
POLITICAL STRATEGIST, AND BEST-SELLING AUTHOR

Dr. Clarice Fluitt is by far one of the most captivating teachers I have ever encountered. She has the unique gift of being able to unpack inspiration and insight in a humorous, inspiring, practical and personal way that few people can accomplish. The wisdom she shares from her incredible life experiences that she includes in her newest book, *Re-Script Your Future*, is simply transformational. She will literally keep you on the edge of your seat and challenge you to rethink your worldview and mindset in ways you never imagined. Through this book, she will move your spirit in a deep and profound way.

KENDRA TODD
"THE APPRENTICE" SEASON THREE WINNER

Acknowledgments

A book is only as good as the team that puts it all together. My team is one of the best. Most people think of teams as a certain core group of individuals, and for the most part, that is true. In the case of this book, my core team was enhanced and the book enriched by those who contributed to it through the telling of their stories and sharing of their testimonies. Romacio, Linda, Diane, and Liam were all major contributors with significant input. Carol Martinez, my Interior Designer, continues to amaze me with her heart of service toward a perfected project. Emery Thibodeaux, my Cover Designer, brings the inspiration that compels the pages to be turned. Dr. Krista Abbott was instrumental in creating and gathering critical material that brought possibility and relevance to each page. Dr. Tandie Mazule, my Executive Assistant, and Dr. Evon Peet, my Administrative Assistant, bring what sometimes looks like blurred impossibilities into clearly defined focus with purpose, intent, and a bar that is set at excellence. The Lord brings the breath of life to each word on every page, and the end result is a book that is relevant, applicable, and of benefit to everyday life.

Table of Contents

Foreword

D r. Clarice's eloquence and warmth underscore her capacity for compassion as she lovingly encourages her readers to closely examine their situations through her newest book *Re-Script Your Future: Power-Packed Proclamations for Your Life, Business, and Government.*

Dr. Clarice Fluitt is one of a kind. A master storyteller who draws from deep reserves of energy and wisdom gained from many years as a pastor and mentor who electrified audiences worldwide. Her character and charisma allow her to connect with a wide range of people, from those on top of the ladder, to those striving to get there.

Dr. Clarice possesses a genuineness of spirit that transforms the mind, touches the heart, and ignites the spirit. I have been blessed to share the stage with her, and I have seen her electrify and mesmerize the audience with her homespun wisdom. She combines practicality and realistic strategies that empower people to transcend difficult situations and live their dreams. In my opinion, Dr. Clarice Fluitt is one of the most powerful orators on the planet today.

I submit to you through the course of this book that you, also, have the ability to affect the course of events in your life, family, business, government, and world in which you live. As you follow the instructions throughout these pages, begin to see yourself as the solution to every situation. *Re-Script Your Future* provides real-world solutions that readers can use to get unstuck and enjoy immediate success in their personal and professional lives.

LES BROWN
MOTIVATIONAL SPEAKER BUSINESS COACH
AND BEST-SELLING AUTHOR

Introduction

This book will enhance your knowledge and understanding of the secrets behind the power of our scriptural proclamations. There is no better place to start than by you, the reader and I, coming together in prayer. Let's invite the Holy Spirit, the Lord and the giver of life, to be our teacher; to lead, guide, and keep us in compliance with God's perfect will. I do believe that you will be enriched by this book.

You will read some wonderful testimonies that will not be testing and moaning, but rather will be victorious words about how God, in His merciful way, gives us His opinion when He says, "If you would just choose to agree with Me."

One of the things that the Lord has revealed to me is the ability to understand that the spoken Word of God carries His power and purpose. My heart's desire is that each and every one of you reading this book will derive the benefit of what I have learned so that you, too, can speak God's wonderful Word over yourself, your family, and all who are a part of the world in which you live.

Let's get started!

Gracious God and Father, I thank You for the opportunity and the privilege to cross pollinate with each of the readers of this book. I declare over each and every one of your children that they are among the fearless, faithful believers of God. They are those who summon and steward the Gospel of grace and glory.

You have given us Your Word, Almighty King, so that we may open our mouth and, like David of long ago when he flung that sling and brought the giant down, Your Word in our mouth becomes a weapon.

You have given us a pure heart and pure motives. We are those who have been forged on the anvil of misunderstanding and persecution. Lord, each of these readers have circumstances and situations that are challenging but, Lord, You never waste a thing. We choose to be grateful people and not waste our sorrows.

We pray for the redeemed to appear in greater authority with consequence in their words.

Devil, we tell you that you are old and ugly. You will never know the love of God. You are totally defeated by the blood of the Lamb of God. Every plot, plan and scheme you have against those who are reading this book, against their finances, families, or health, I declare to be broken in Jesus' name. Open their hearts for the revelation of Your victory over all the powers of darkness.

Father, I thank You for making us hungry for Your presence, power, and the sound of Your voice. As we learn about these powerful secrets of proclaiming Your holy Word, may the reality of Your righteousness become real to each and every one of us. We pray this in Jesus' mighty wonderful name. Amen.

1

Understand the Power that the Word of God Carries

In learning about the secrets behind the power of scripturally prayed proclamations, we should understand their significance. According to the Dictionary of Bible Themes, there are 5,463 proclamations in the Bible. The fundamental definition of a proclamation is to make a clear declaration of something.[1]

The purpose of a spoken proclamation is to empower the obedient so that we become not just hearers of the Word, but doers, also. We learn that a proclamation is the spoken faith filled word of agreement with God.

For example, if I were to pray, "Oh Lord God, someday I just pray that I will be able to know Your voice." This is faithless begging, not a prayer.

---

1 (https://www.biblegateway.com/resources/dictionary-of-bible-themes/5463-proclamations)

According to the Word of God, John 10:4-5 says,

"And when He brings out His own sheep, He goes before them; and the sheep follow Him, for *they know His voice*. Yet they will by no means follow a stranger, but will flee from him, for they do not know the voice of strangers" (NKJV – emphasis added).

Although you may not feel that you hear His voice, do not disagree with the Word of God. Your carnal mind may still be in the process of being transformed through the renewing of your mind by the Word of God.

As we begin our prayer life, we often ask God to do what His Word says He has already done. We discover that we must pray, speak, and proclaim His Word as we agree with Him.

The Word of God teaches me that I do hear His voice. So, my prayer needs to line up with God's Word. I will pray, "Lord, thank You that I hear You. Thank You, God, that I hear Your voice. I am led by Your Spirit." As I begin to agree with God, my faith is increased. Without faith, it is impossible to please God. Remember, you are creating when you say, "Well, I just don't hear the voice of God." Or, "I could never speak in tongues. I could not prophesy. I don't have this ability." Your words begin to testify against the Word of God.

The word "salvation" is a translation. The original word actually means "I am healed, I am delivered, and I am prosperous." If I say with my mouth, "I am sick, I am oppressed, and I am poor," I have empowered the demonic forces because my ear hears my voice and believes my voice above all other voices. That voice, then, goes into my thought life, and my thought life begins to agree with a lie. So, I have a thought, I have a word, I have an action. Either I am choosing to release life, or death, with my mouth.

One of the things we have to understand is that we have the privilege and responsibility to learn what the Bible actually says. There are many people who choose to agree with fact, not truth. They say, "You know, the doctor says I have this, and the doctor says I have that." And, you may actually have it as a fact. I know what it is to have complications as I had to undergo a hip replacement even though I walked by faith for a supernatural healing for many years. Some of you have heard my testimony. I have experienced some incredible healings in my own home, and know about the power of healing and deliverance. I could tell you story after story after story of the healing power of God. [2]

When this health situation came in my life and I was diagnosed with avascular necrosis, which is where the

2 My book, *Ridiculous Miracles*, gives many accounts of miracles I have witnessed in my home and ministry around the world. Find it on Amazon.com

bone does not get a blood supply resulting in the actual death of the bone, I had no fear of it. Whenever I walked it was bone on bone and very painful. Yet I had no apprehension because I know the voice of God that says, "You are healed."

Prior to my hip replacement surgery, God, in His mercy, wanted to take me into a deeper comprehension and understanding of being led by His Spirit. So, I prayed, and had people pray with me. I confessed, "I'm healed." I said, "This is a lying spirit."

I was choosing to be faithful and refused to be moved by my situations. But you see, God wants to take us from glory to glory and increase our faith. I heard the Lord speak to me clearly. He said, "I want you to trust Me with another degree of trust." So, I asked the Lord about this hip and healing situation. He said, "You must continue to say with your mouth, 'I am the healed. I am the delivered. I am the prosperous. No weapon formed against me can prosper.'"

Proclamations = Information = Revelation

Whenever you are audibly speaking the Word of God remember that your voice has a frequency which will stimulate your ears. And, your ears will transmit this frequency to your brain. When this happens, your mind becomes renewed and you hit what we might refer to as a critical mass of information, and that revelation begins to agree with God on the things that are absolutely yours.

As I began to say, "I am His. Righteousness, eternal victory, and deliverance are all mine; I am an heir and a joint heir with Jesus," there came a time when that information was transformed into revelation. That information reached into my heart and became revelation. I was learning that information without revelation produces imitation that leads to stagnation.

This kind of revelation cannot be earned or learned. It comes through the empowering Holy Ghost, Lord and giver of life. When my intention was to know God; when I was not after the things of God, but rather the God of things, revelation opened up, went down into my heart, and all apprehension about how God wanted to manifest my healing was gone.

I went to a wonderful doctor who was just delightful. We prayed together and I continued to make the declaration that I would not be fearful of this surgery. We learn patience through the things that we suffer. I went through the surgery and had an incredible outcome. I am now walking pain-free. I do not believe that my choice to have surgery was God's second best. In prayer, the Holy Spirit reminded me that Luke was a doctor and a great friend to Jesus. Doctors are a gift from God.

Proclamations = Information = Revelation = Transformation

Moving into the fullness of making proclamations that bring particular manifestation comes through the revelation of the finished work of Christ, where nothing is done out of fear, but by faith and love. As we choose to proclaim that the only thing we are allowed to fear is God and God alone, His Word is no longer merely *informing* us, but is *transforming* us because it has become revelatory. Then, out of the abundance of our heart, our mouth begins to speak truth.

Most have read about the prayer of Jabez from the Book of Chronicles. Jabez had come to a point in his life where he just needed the Lord to bless him. He was an honorable man who began to call on God. This is a proclamation in which a man's heart is revealed. He is not doing a ritualistic thing. He has not memorized anything. He just simply poured his heart out and called on the God of Israel saying, "Oh, that You would bless me indeed, and enlarge my territory, that Your hand would be with me, and that You would keep me from evil, that I may not cause pain! So God granted him what he requested" (1 Chronicles 4:10 NKJV).

Jabez's prayer was very similar to the Lord's prayer: "Lead me not into temptation, but deliver me from evil."

Proclamations = Information = Revelation =Transformation = Manifestation

God granted to Jabez what he requested. I do not know how much God enlarged his territory, and I do not know the specifics of how the hand of God was on Jabez. But I do know this: The Word of God says you have not because you ask not. Learning how to approach without reproach is very significant and important. Understand that what God watches over to perform are His words (Jeremiah 1:12 NKJV).

You and I should learn to open our mouths. We are not poor banished children of Eve. We are the sons and daughters of the living God. We are redeemed from the curse of the law of sin and death. Our names are written in the Lamb's Book of Life. You will begin to say, "There is more to me than what you see." Suddenly, courage, strength, and God's faith begin to rise up in you. Life draws life.

When I open my mouth and speak the Word of God, I see my mouth like a launching pad of something more powerful than nuclear warheads because I have learned to speak the Word of God. I have learned to proclaim and say what I want because my wants have been changed. Now, I delight to do the will of God, and God gives me the desires of my heart.

I learned about making proclamations. I have a very diverse spiritual background. I was reared in a Baptist home and became Methodist and then Episcopalian. After that I became Presbyterian. Then I married a Catholic. So, I became Catholic. And throughout all of that my quest, what I was looking for, was to find the God of power and love. I just could not seem to lock into the power of God. In the fullness of time, I came to the understanding that it is not the title you carry, but what is in your heart.

2

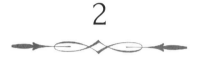

Do Not Pray the Problem; Pray the Word of God

I'd like to introduce you to Liam. Liam is a coaching client of mine who has an incredible testimony, and has given me his permission to share his story with you. Liam is a young man from Bournemouth, England. He is a teacher by profession and loves the Lord. Yet he suffered serious heart problems that, without God, would have left his future very bleak.

"I had been on Easter vacation and was preparing to go back to work. It was a Sunday night. Suddenly, my heart went into absolute chaos. My family called the ambulance and I was rushed to the hospital. My heart was going so crazy that they were worried about the treatment they could give me because of further complications and risks of stroke. All the while this was going on, I was remarkably at peace. My body was doing chaotic things, but my spirit was strong. I felt so close to God. His presence seemed so there. It was 1:00 a.m. in the morning. I was still smiling and talking to the nurses and telling them about God and the love of Jesus, and sharing all these wonderful things.

"They kept me in the hospital until I was ready enough to be discharged. But, once I left the hospital, I was then sent to my family physician. The doctor said to me, 'Basically, what you need to do is make sure you exercise, build up your strength, and take some time off work.' He told me that I needed to go swimming. Now, I haven't swum for I don't know how many years. I swim when I'm on holiday, and that's about it. So, I thought, 'Well, I need to bring some discipline in here.' I signed up at my local swimming center and thought, 'Now I'm going to see what happens.'

"The doctor put me on some medication as well. So, I went swimming and was about halfway down the pool when I realized I couldn't go any further. I was watching all these people next to me who were obviously regular swimmers going up and down, up and down, up and down. I just stood there feeling a little bit frustrated. I walked my way back to the other end of the pool and thought, 'You know what? I'm just going to pray about this.' So, I prayed. I started praying in tongues and thanking the Lord that I am His child. I started thanking Him that we are people who are living in a natural body, but we are supernatural beings; we are spirit beings. I said, 'Dear Lord, what do I do here?' And He said, 'Remember what you have learned about proclamations.'

"I said, 'Okay, yes, thank You Lord.' So, I started proclaiming. I said, 'Now body, you listen to me. This is how it's going to be. Arms and legs, you are going to do what you need to do. Heart, you are going to pump really well here. And lungs, you are going to breathe. And on top of that, this is going to be the easiest swim we have ever done in our lives.' And I thanked the Lord. I thanked Him there and then. I took off in the water and I did one length, then two lengths, then three, and four lengths all the while praising God. When I got home that evening, I e-mailed Dr. Clarice and said, 'It works. It works. It works. This is wonderful.'

'The power of that was such a revelation at that point. Dr. Clarice then told me, 'You know, information which is not carried out becomes an imitation; but, if you actually get a revelation of these things, it is absolutely wonderful. When that happens, you then realize that, "if my proclamation works here, then my proclamation will work there."

"It was amazing to see that, and it has been so wonderful to see God now working in many other ways, both for me and my family as well.

"When I went back to the doctor, he asked me how I had been getting along. After he examined my heart, he said, 'Oh, I'm looking at a heart that has no problems.

Your heart is functioning well. It's absolutely perfect.' And again, it was just that morning that I had proclaimed, 'Heart. Listen to me. You are going to do well. You are blessed and highly favored of the Lord.'

"An additional story that has to do with proclamations is about my sister. She has had a muscle condition for the last 10 years and is only one of two in the entire United Kingdom with this type of condition. In the natural, it eats away at the ligaments and destroys them. She has been to various hospitals and the Clinical Trials Office (CTO) in London. About two or three months ago, the CTO said, 'You're just getting weaker and weaker and weaker.'

"I took my sister to the CTO. I'd noticed that she seemed to be a lot better. Again, of course, we had been proclaiming the Word of God. When she came out of the CTO, she had this big smile on her face. And I said, 'What is it?' She said, 'The physio said that I have muscles growing.' I said, 'Sorry, what is that?' She said, 'There are muscles that are naturally just appearing in my shoulders, in my back, and in my arms.' That is still continuing to this day. We praise God because He is doing a creative miracle."

What an incredible testimony that builds faith for anyone in need of healing, deliverance, or the manifestation of financial provision. I proclaim this is your season to release God's Word.

3

The Things of God Become Yours by the Reason of Use

I pray I will have great success in the teaching aspect of this book.

Gracious God and Father, You are the healer. Your Word in Mark 11:24 says that, "Therefore, I say to you, whatever things you ask when you pray, believe that you receive them, and you will have them." So, I begin to proclaim right now with the Word of God that comes forth and says, "You have not because you ask not." Lord, forgive us for forgetting to ask.

Right now, I ask that the wonderful provision which has been made for health, healing, and wholeness be released upon each and every person reading this book. I proclaim health, wealth, joy, peace, comprehension, and understanding. I thank You for the wonderful people reading these pages, and bless each and every one of them. In Jesus' name, I pray.

Attitude of Gratitude

It is a joy unspeakable when we realize how God does such amazing things, gives us new life, and sets us here on this earth to become a part of His body. He revealed His plan of salvation for us, not just to be born, but to be born again of the Spirit of God and become as righteous as God by having faith in what Jesus has done. God not only loved us enough to let us be born, but to let us be born again; to be sons of God.

The Bible says we are heirs and joint heirs of all things with Jesus Christ. When we look at circumstances and situations in this world, we are tempted to believe that the facts are the truth when, actually, they are not. Everything God had to say, He said through His Word.

Proclamations

Proclamations of the Word of God are our tools that bring manifestation.

As I watched my house being built, I was amazed at the kind of tools that were needed. I remember one day, right when they were about to begin to build, when I came to the lot. There was this enormous machine that was bringing dirt and pouring it all over the place. I thought we had enough dirt but, you know, when you start building a firm foundation, the things that you thought were enough, aren't always enough. In the same way, we are God's house and He will begin to establish a firm foundation and fill us with His Word inside of our hearts.

I believe proclaiming the Word of God is like tools that can literally cause the truth of the heavenly reign of God to be brought from heaven to earth. Scripture says, 'Thy will be done in earth as it is in heaven.'

Proclamations manifest heaven on earth.

As we begin to proclaim the Word of God and not just our opinions, hopes or wishes, we must be biblically oriented to say the Word of God so that the whole world will come into the revelation of the finished work of Jesus Christ.

Nothing purposed against God's spoken Word has any valid rights or objections to come against the believer. Biblical proclamations are the same as the will and the purpose of God. We must begin to understand the privilege, power, and authority that God entrusted to us in administrating the estate of God from the revelation of a finished work. When we begin to proclaim our vision and say things that we are seeing in our life, and begin to say what we think we want, we create confusion. But, when we begin to proclaim God's Word and release His purpose into our lives, instead of confusion there is clarity.

Releasing and Establishing the Will and Purpose of God

When a believer proclaims, "I am blessed" according to Psalm 112:1, and establishes God's blessings while separating himself from anything that has purposed against God's blessing, he literally begins to destroy darkness and evil plans as God's Word is released as light. When God's Word, which is light, "a lamp unto my feet, a light unto my path," shows up, darkness has a nervous breakdown as we begin to say, "It is written, it is written, it is written."

At some time in our lives we have probably experienced some anxiety, fears, doubts, dread, or pain. We have a millisecond to decide whether we will agree with what we are feeling, or respond with the Word of God. My five senses, if left unchecked, will react with memories from the old nature. If you are a born again believer, you do not have an old nature, but you do have a memory. That is why we are being transformed, changed, metamorphized through the renewing of our mind by pulling down these strongholds, vain imaginations, and every high thing that exalts itself against the Word of God. Proclamations are a powerful tool to do this.

We see these areas of our life where we are still having some negative conversations about ourselves, our life, what we look like, talk like, or act like. We are equipped and commissioned with divine light. A proclamation can be a harsh judgment imposed on a defeated enemy that cannot oppose what you say.

When believers proclaim, "I am blessed. I am healed. I am above and not beneath," then light comes out of their mouths. Darkness cannot stay in the presence of light. God's blessings literally separate that person from anything that is purposed against it. The destruction of darkness and evil plans happens as you speak the Word of God.

Savior, healer, mighty God, angels, all of them are backing you up when you call on the name of Jesus. When you proclaim God's Word, when you agree with God and proclaim His promises, you are speaking God's blessing on your own life. You are releasing and establishing the will and purpose of God. We begin to separate the deceit and lying plans of the enemy off our family, children, uncles, aunts, all of our family members. God's unit of measure for salvation is a household. Our responsibility is to keep our confession over our household and not allow the accuser to influence our faith in God's promise.

From the Old Testament to the New Testament, we see God again and again working in the family and, as you get one person born again, you can get the whole family if your mouth is right. Don't say, "Oh, you know, old John has been a rebel all of his life. He has been in jail. He has done this, or that." Do not talk like that, but instead begin to create with the fruit of your lips. Speak the Word of God and proclaim that your whole family is coming in to the Kingdom of God. Proclaim the goodness of God, and that all of your children are disciples taught of the Lord, and great is their peace and undisturbed composure.

I trust that you are getting as excited as I am about this. The proclamations that you speak are actually imposing a judgment like a court order on the enemy, and he cannot oppose the Word of God. He can oppose your word and my word, but when we are standing with a helmet of salvation and the breastplate of righteousness, our loins girded with the word of truth, and our feet shod with the preparation of the gospel of peace, we can defeat any enemy.

We have the sword of the Spirit and the shield of faith. We walk like God, talk like God, act like God, think like God, and the only way the enemy can distinguish you from God is when you open your mouth and say something that does not align with God's Word. When you do that, you make a judgment on yourself or others. We have life and death in our mouth. This is the power of a biblical proclamation.

Recognize the Weight and Power Behind the Godly Words that You Are Speaking

As surely as Jesus has taken our place in heaven, He has commissioned and empowered us to take His place on the earth. So, we have to keep that full armor on, put a guard over our tongue, and begin to pray in tongues more than you have ever prayed before. The Bible was not given to us to only read through. It is so powerful when you speak the Word of God. The Scripture shows us that, in the beginning, God did not think us into existence. The Scripture says God said, 'Let there be light; let there be an unveiling of what's already here.' We must learn that we are made in the image and the likeness of God, and are created to proclaim the Word of God.

Some of you may remember the story of the great prophet, Ezekiel. Ezekiel was looking out over a valley of dead, dry, separated bones. It was an impossible situation. God asked him this question, "Can these bones live again?" Ezekiel replied with, 'Lord, You know. I'm just a young man here. I don't know if they can live again, but You know.' The Word of the Lord came to Ezekiel, and God said, 'Prophesy, oh man of God. Make proclamations under the inspiration of My Spirit. You talk, and I'll breathe.'

The Spirit of God is released when we begin to understand that the will of God is always creative, but it is the Word of God that activates His creativity. Somebody on

35

the face of this earth is going to have to agree with God and speak in power, and in determination that you have a firm purpose. Speak with authority, direction, intention, and conviction, and recognize the weight and power behind the godly words that you are speaking.

According to the Word of God, you can either be positive or negative. You can make a decision about what you want to do. Proclaiming God's Word makes changes in both the spiritual and physical realm. Jesus said, 'The words that you speak are spirit and life.' You create with your words by speaking forth God's Word. God's Word will not return void, but will accomplish what it is sent forth to do (Isaiah 55:11 NKJV). You have to send out the Word. You have to be willing to speak the Word of God.

We Are the Voice of His Word

Hebrews 4:16 says that, as the redeemed, we are to come boldly before the throne of God. We are not to creep in as though there is something wrong with us. We are coming as the righteousness of God because our faith is in Christ. He has given us robes of righteousness. Our proclamations release and commission angels. I have so many stories about that. Psalm 103:20 says, "Bless the Lord, you His angels, who excel in strength, who do His word, heeding the voice of His word" (NKJV).

We are the voice of His Word. We are the body of Christ. We are the anointed of God and the agents that He has chosen to live in. The voice of God is the voice of many waters, and you and I are filled with the living waters of God. When you open your mouth and begin to proclaim the Word of God, you create a flood of love, life, healing, and deliverance, and darkness has a nervous breakdown.

We cannot just think about these good things, we have to begin to say them. We have to learn about the power in making proclamations, and the difference between prophesying, and praying. They all serve a very similar purpose but are different in their approach. God will bring all of this understanding about prayer, supplication, and intercession to you. The purpose of this book is not to discuss so much the aspect of prayer, but to let you know the difference between prayer, and proclamations.

They both have great power. Prayer is a solemn request for help including an expression of thanksgiving to God. You can have intercession for others but talking to God, rather than talking at Him, has to be born of a relationship. What God is desiring is intimacy, union, and communion.

The things of God
become yours by the
reason of use.

4

Aligning Yourself with God's Word

One day I received a call from a gentleman from the Congo. He is a minister and prophet, and had seen me on Sid Roth's program, "It's Supernatural." There are people that you have an immediate witness in your spirit with when you hear their voice, and see who they are. He said, "I knew you could help me if I could just get in touch with you. I have a terrible problem. I go out, heal the sick, and do all of the things that Jesus commissioned. But, when I come back home, I am filled with sorrow and just don't have any joy." I had never met him, did not know anything about him, and could barely understand his accent. I spoke the following words, "In the authority of the holy name of Jesus our Lord and Savior, I proclaim the joy of the Lord upon you. I rebuke this foolish spirit of grief and proclaim that you are full of joy."

The next thing I heard on that phone was hysterical laughter; holy laughter. He laughed, and laughed, and laughed. He said, "You must come to Congo." I said, "Well, you're just going to have to be my Congo, son. We are going to have to talk a while about this."

The nine gifts of the Holy Spirit are broken down into the word of knowledge, wisdom, the discerning of spirits, tongues, interpretation of tongues, prophecy, faith, miracles, and healing. These gifts have been given for the building of the body of Christ.

What you and I received is the Holy Spirit. Whatever God has a need for you and me to do, is included in the gifts of the Spirit. The things of God become yours by the reason of use. Let me say that again, the things of God become yours by the reason of use. The Bible says that we are to covet, desire, seek, and practice spiritual things. You are going to have to do all of that in regard to making your proclamations of faith.

I would like to introduce you to Romacio, another friend of mine who has an incredible testimony. His story, in his own words, goes like this:

"We all know that you cannot help somebody who does not want to be helped. At other times, you may desire to help a person but they do not understand your style. Dr. Clarice's style is something that resonates with me tremendously, and has made a huge impact on my life.

"I'll take you back really quickly. Three or four years ago I had gotten to a point in my life where, I guess a simple way of saying it is, I had done the very best that I could with what I knew. I needed something supernatural to happen. I needed something more.

"I grew up in the church. It has always been an important part of my life. I knew about God from being in church every Sunday, every Friday, and again every Thursday for choir rehearsal. I grew up in East Oakland, California; not the best of areas, so church was the place that my parents chose to keep us at a lot. That's where I grew up and spent the majority of my time.

"But I got to a point in my life where I needed something supernatural. I had big goals and big dreams; I wanted more for my life. I had done the best that I could with what I knew, but I needed something more. I want to be honest with you. One of the biggest things that I did not like about Christians and professing believers was that, although they claimed to have been believing for 30 or 40 years, they were still broke, still sick, and it seemed that everything in their life was going wrong. There was nothing about their life or lifestyle that was compelling me to want to sign up for that class, if you follow what I'm saying.

"There I was, knowing I needed something. At this point and time in my life, I knew about God, but had never had a true relationship with Him. There were some negative things that had happened in my life. I want to underline the word negative because sometimes what we see as a negative, or bad situation, is actually the thing that God uses to get your attention. Some negative things had happened to me, and I knew at that point that I needed something supernatural to take place.

"I remember driving down to see my mother. I told her that I really was at a point where I wanted to understand this God that I knew about, but really did not know at all. I would always say, "I love God," but I had no context, and no relationship with Him. To have a relationship with someone means you have to spend time with them. I never had a real relationship with Him. I remember telling my mom about this. She gave me some assignments to do. And then one day I was on an airplane and met Dr. Fluitt. We struck up a conversation. It's kind of funny that the moment you begin to put out into the spiritual realm what your desires are, and what you are in need of, I believe you will always find what you are looking for.

"There I was on an airplane, with a woman I had never met, who was about 35 years my senior, and who was just being her loving self. It was only after we connected and I found out who she was, and that she was a spiritual advisor to many, that I simply said to her, 'I want to know more about God.' I remember thinking to myself, 'Wow. This is exactly what I'm looking for.'

I signed up for her courses, and began to allow her to personally mentor me. We would talk once a week for about an hour. I would have my pen and paper and would take notes. Many times, things that she was saying would go over my head. But I was determined to create a relationship with God. I had a lot of sin in my life, thought God probably would not want anything to do with me, and figured I would be the last person God would want to talk to.

"My biggest fear came with the thought that, after establishing this relationship with God, I would make mistakes, or neglect to honor my commitments to Him. That was the biggest fear that kept me for years from engaging in a relationship. I did not know how to deal with the doubt, or the shame.

"Week after week she would mentor me as I took copious notes and asked questions. I cannot say that I understood every single thing she said within that hour, but I can tell you that every time we talked, I was present; I was there; I was wanting. My heart desired to learn how to do this relationship thing with God. I thank God for her style. She was so gentle, yet firm and funny. She was real, not one of those people that are so heavenly minded they are no earthly good; too high and mighty they can't really relate.

"Every week I was fully engaged, taking notes, eager to learn, and I began to get better. She got a chance to know me, and I got a chance to know her. What an amazing relationship it has been. She is the one who taught me the power of proclamations. I knew that what I wanted in life was to be very successful. There was a particular monetary dollar amount that was my goal. Let me say that I am not giving this testimony to brag, and am no better than anyone reading this book; but I can tell you that, if this worked for me, I know with absolute certainty it will work for you. This goes far and beyond naming and claiming.

"I began to really pursue a relationship with God. I knew that money was a necessary tool to live out your life's purpose. I knew that; I believed that. I believe that money is very important. I remember before I signed up with Dr. Fluitt, praying a very serious prayer to God. I said, 'Listen, if I'm going to sign up for Your course, God, I don't want to be like other people that I've seen. They say they believe in You, but nothing about their life reflects believing at all. They're still stuck in the same rut, month after month, year after year. If I'm going to sign up for Your class, I want the world to see the manifestation of Your glory through my life; through my deeds. I want the world to see it.' I said, 'God, I promise You, I will give it my best. I already know I'm going to make some mistakes, but I will give it my best.'

"And I did. I knew my ultimate goal was to be able to tithe one million dollars per year, which would be 10% of

44

$10 million earned. I wanted to be able to one day give away a million dollars per year to various small businesses, or people that were trying to do business throughout the world. That is what I wanted to do. Now, I have to tell you, I have not yet made $10 million a year, but I know it's definitely on the way.

"Dr. Fluitt began to teach me about proclamations, what they meant, and how this really works. Let me just tell you what I have learned. I am not saying that I am her perfect student, but I can tell you, this man has come a long way. I have learned that satan comes to steal, kill, and destroy. That is straight from the Word and, finally, is crystal clear in my brain. So, what does that mean? A lot of the times I would self-sabotage. They say that doubt is worse than fear. I was so doubtful. I couldn't do this; it's not going to work; what if this; what if that. I was just so doubtful.

"I am so glad that I have now learned how to deal with the enemy of doubt. We were all created in God's image; that's a fact. I now know that doubt is, literally, a demonic force that is worse than fear.

"What I said to God is this, 'Hey, listen, if I'm going to follow You, what I want is to have unbelievable faith.' Remember, when I first got started, I said to Dr. Fluitt, 'My goal is to have unbelievable faith. How do you do that?" She began to tell me that faith is like a muscle. It only grows by reason of use. I said, "Okay, that sounds cute. But how do we make it grow?" She began to teach me some things. One of the things she taught me was the power of a proclamation.

"I learned that when you are proclaiming, you are aligning yourself with God's Word. Let me break that down. Basically, God's Word does not lie. When I talk about wanting to increase my faith, I have to align myself with what His Word says. This is powerful, but it is also hard when you are broke, busted, and disgusted, things not going the way you want them to go. You have to align yourself with God's Word whether you believe it or not.

"What I have learned in my short relationship with God thus far is that God does not respond to yelling and screaming. Believe it or not, He does not even respond to tears. He responds to written plans and responds to your faith. When she taught me the power of proclamations, I wrote proclamations that I say every single day, and they go like this:"

I, Romacio, proclaim that I have a vision for divine provision.

I am an end-time financier and a marketplace minister.

46

As a marketplace person, I have the privilege and the biblical responsibility to tithe, to give offerings, and to support the Kingdom of God.

As a marketplace minister, I know that this calling includes and goes beyond the boundaries of a local church.

As a marketplace minister, I will concentrate on influencing and transforming key components of society. This includes education, media, entertainment, government, arts, and commerce. These are the areas that I will be a part of changing and transforming to bring an understanding of the revelation of God.

Proverbs 18:15 tells me that I am a candidate to increase in wisdom and wealth.

I choose to guard my heart with all diligence.

I proclaim that poverty is a curse and cannot come down my dwelling.

The Word of God and the epistle of 3 John teaches that it is the will of God that above all things He desires that I prosper and be of health as my soul prospers.

I speak to my body, I speak to my soul, and I speak to my spirit. I proclaim wholeness into my life.

I proclaim that money is an important tool that will enable me to accomplish those great and mighty things that God has called and created me to do.

Money magnifies what is in my heart, and what is in my heart is God.

Money is the course that I need to enforce and activate the will of God.

Money is to serve the call of God.

According to Matthew 6:24, money is a tool for global harvest.

According to Philippians 4:15-17, money will expose a spirit of poverty.

According to Deuteronomy 8:18, God gives me the power to get wealth.

I am a man of breakthrough.

According to Micah 2:13, I am a divine radical who pursues the purpose of God for supernatural favor and financial breakthrough.

I have been created to promote and support the cause of Christ.

I am a forceful and faithful man of God.

I am called, and I am equipped to invest in missions and send the gospel around the world.

I am generous to the poor and to the needy.

My God takes delight in my prosperity.

I proclaim that my God is more than enough.

His name is El Shaddai; He is more than enough.

I proclaim, now that I have broken through into the dimension of multiplication, I repeat, I proclaim now that I have broken through into the dimension of multiplication, I have the spirit of generosity and mammon has no hold upon me.

I proclaim I have supernatural favor according to Luke 6:38.

I proclaim that giving to God opens the gate of unlimited, unrealistic favor that will flow into my life according to Proverbs 8:16.

"Those are the proclamations that I try to read every single day, regardless of how I feel, to keep me aligned with what I expect."

Those of you who are reading this book need to remember that when Romacio made these proclamations and they were established, it was not just information, but it became revelation. Revelation which cannot be earned or learned comes from fellowship in the Holy Ghost to show you that the Word of God has the power to perform itself. It just needs to be released. That is what God has given us a mouth for. Every river has a mouth, and we are the river of God.

Knowing all of this, Romacio has been able, with his proclamations, to earn millions of dollars that he is using to help so many people. It is an incredible thing that God was able to do, once this young man made up his mind to move in the direction of agreeing with God. The main thing that we want to be able to do is to hear, agree with God, and create with the fruit of our lips by calling the things that are not to become the things that arc.

My hope is that each of my readers will tailor-make their own personal proclamations that align with the Word of God. You may not be called to be a multi-millionaire. That might not be your vision. I had a situation where my daughter was bound by drugs. It looked so bad, but after 27 years of saying over and over and over again, "All of my children are disciples taught of the Lord, and great is their peace and undisturbed composure," things began to turn around. Even though I did not have the revelation of it in the beginning, over the years, it became reality to me. As you form your own proclamation, back it up with the Word of God and you will see the goodness of the Lord.

Supernatural Supply

"For My thoughts are not your thoughts, Nor are your ways My ways," says the Lord. "For as the heavens are higher than the earth, so are My ways higher than your ways, and My thoughts than your thoughts" (Isaiah 55:8-9 NKJV).

"And my God shall supply all your need according to His riches in glory by Christ Jesus" (Philippians 4:19 NKJV).

"And now, Lord, what do I wait for? My hope is in You" (Psalm 39:7 NKJV).

Diane is a 69 year old divorced woman who was a caretaker for her 93 year old mother She had learned to trust and rely on the Lord over the years. She is called to marketplace ministry through business as an entrepreneur, and believes she is to receive great wealth. But the process getting there had been arduous and long!

Diane lost a new business she had started due to an emergency medical situation that cost her $30,000. She had no insurance at the time, and very little money. Everything went downhill financially after that.

When she learned about my upcoming teleconference, she signed up for it. She only had about $25 to her name but she felt the Lord would take care of everything. She said she had very much enjoyed hearing me on Sid Roth's show and YouTube, and reading my book *Experiencing the Power of God's Word*. She was led by the Holy Spirit, by faith, to sign up and pay the cost for the conference.

It was during the second session when I concluded teaching on the power of God's Word I encouraged the participants to share if they had anything they wanted to share. Diane responded and said, "This very day I have been served with legal papers to appear in court in 30 days regarding the foreclosure of my home. It is a very trying time. I have owned my home for 16 years..."

After Diane shared her situation, I immediately prayed for her, proclaiming God's powerful Word over her life and present situation. That was the last I heard about it until several months later, when she sent me her testimony. Allow me to share!

This is her testimony: :

"You prayed for me that night a powerful prayer. It was a great blessing and gave me courage.

"I was going to have to appear in court in August, so I was praying, believing, proclaiming. I attempted to apply for a modification with the Lender but it was later denied. I needed around $6,000 to catch up on my mortgage payments and for my loan to be reinstated. The days passed by and seemingly there was no change.

My court date was fast approaching.

"Meantime, at your next teleconference, you said the Lord wanted you to prophesy over us mainly regarding finances. And you did that. So, after you sent the MP3 recording of the meeting, I transcribed every word of that prayer and prophecy you gave over us. And I began to speak out loud proclaiming what you said word for word, daily, in addition to the scriptures that I had already been proclaiming over my life.

"The time for the court hearing came. Nothing in the natural had changed. I called the Lender's attorneys to try to get the court hearing continued. But they said no, that it was not possible. They didn't have the authorization to do that, and so I would have to appear in court.

"First breakthrough (August): When I arrived at the Clerk of Superior Court's office for the hearing, the Lender's attorney did not show up! While we were waiting for this attorney, their office called and said the attorney would not be there, and told the Clerk to continue the hearing at a later date! The Clerk could have continued it for just 30 days, but she said she was going to continue it for the maximum amount of 60 days which would put it in October! I was elated and very thankful. It gave me more time to try to come up with the finances I needed. More time to decree and declare!

"By now, we had finished your teleconference series but I was still proclaiming like a crazy, determined woman, not only your proclamations, but also the ones I had written!

"Next breakthrough (later in August): Someone casually mentioned to me that there was money available for people who had any damage due to a recent storm we had. They suggested that I should apply if I needed it. She did not know I had some water come into my sunroom which actually had done some damage. I never, ever considered or thought of the possibility of me receiving aid like that, and had never applied for anything in the past. But long story short: I did call about it, was sent an application, and was approved for a $40,000 grant that I did not have to pay back. I was blown away.

"I was so encouraged and said to the Lord, "You must be planning to provide for me to get out of foreclosure since You just provided this huge grant!"

"At the end of August another God thing: I was going through my mail and throwing away "junk" mail when I heard the Holy Spirit say, "Wait. Don't throw that away." I said, "What, Lord?" And He said, "Look again." So, I went back and picked up the junk mail I had just thrown away and there was something from the State Housing Agency. I'd seen those same things come through the mail year after year. It was an agency that helped people with

mortgage payment problems. And once, a few years back, I even called about it. It was about loans for people who qualified. Number one, I didn't want a loan; and secondly, I didn't meet the criteria. So, whenever they came through the mail, I threw them away.

"But this time I felt the Lord said to call again. I did. They instructed me to contact one of their offices nearest me. Throughout the state independent agencies were hired by the state to do the paperwork. So, they gave me the name of the agent who was about an hour away and she set up a meeting with me.

"*September 5:* I attended the first meeting with the Director of the Housing Agency. I had with me all the paperwork regarding the foreclosure, hearing date, even the modification application which I had already submitted to the Lender. By now, I was in need of ten or eleven thousand dollars' worth of mortgage payments.

"It turned out that the Director was a Christian lady; but, after looking at all my paperwork, she was not optimistic. She said that she would help me try to get the modification through but that, basically, there was no grant money left. She told me that almost every person who had applied for help in the last two months had been denied. Needless to say, that was pretty hard to hear. But then I thought, well Lord, You did have me go this route. There's gotta be a reason.

We finished our meeting and I felt the Lord telling me to pray for her. I asked her if I could, and she was very open. So, I prayed. I was still in a "zone" because of my mother's passing, having just had her homegoing the day before, but the Lord gave me a prophetic word for the Director.

"The Lord revealed to me that the old building we were in was a former hospital and there were spirits in there that needed to go. I asked her if indeed the building used to be a hospital. She was shocked and said, "Yes, how did you know?" I told her about what the Lord revealed to me and began to drive away any evil spirits. She needed healing, so I prayed for healing for her. She also received the baptism of the Holy Spirit right there in that office and spoke in tongues for about 30 minutes!

"Finally, she told me that several of the workers there had been suffering depression and were on medication. We prayed again and I believe depression left that place along with all the demons!

"I believe Jesus did a lot that day. But on the drive home I said, 'Lord, was all of this for that lady and the other folks there? What about my house?' Don't get me wrong, I live to bless people. I was thrilled for the Lord to move in such a way, but I still needed help!

"Around September 7: Meanwhile, another unexpected event arose. I learned that I had not received an insurance

payment for something that happened previously to my house; something pretty insignificant actually. I had filed a claim earlier just because someone in the insurance office suggested I do it but had forgotten about it. But, I got a call from the insurance company saying they had a check for me. I was shocked really. It was for $7,500. An unexpected blessing!

"*October:* The Housing Director called and said the modification I had applied for was denied and there was nothing she could do. So, I asked if I could still fill out the application for a housing grant. She said yes, but again, to please not expect anything. She didn't want me to be disappointed. So, she emailed the application to me.

"*Mid-October:* After filling out the application, the Director sent it out. Within a week there was a response! She called me and was shocked and ecstatic to tell me that I had been preapproved for a grant! A grant that I did not have to pay back! This immediately stopped the foreclosure process, and the hearing date was discontinued until further notice! I was amazed. Within another few days, I had been informed that I was approved for almost $17,000.00 to be paid directly to my Lender.

"*Mid-November just before Thanksgiving:* The back mortgage payments were brought current including all the county taxes and insurance. It even paid almost two months extra in mortgage payments! About then, I received a letter from the Lender's attorneys informing me that all proceedings against me had been stopped. What an awesome Thanksgiving and Christmas!

"Early November: Another unexpected drama! I received a collection letter from the IRS regarding $10,000.00 in back taxes that I owed which occurred when I lost my business. They were demanding payment in full. I have been able to pay current yearly taxes as I file my tax returns, but I just hadn't had enough to catch up with those three years when I lost my business. And now they were demanding payment in full. I talked to the Lord. I said, "I know You are going to help me. You've brought me this far with such blessings." I just continued praying and proclaiming certain scriptures He would bring to mind, and I would make proclamations over the situation along with those I had transcribed from the teleconferences.

"After a few days, the Lord prompted me to look at the collection letter which I had already filed away again. I knew by now to do just what the Lord said. When I reread it, I noticed at the bottom in small print something about a tax advocate. I'd never heard of it. I went to the IRS website to see if I could find out anything about it. It turns out each state has at least one independent IRS tax advocate office. I found a number to call, but they were too busy to handle my account so they forwarded me to a different office.

"Long story short: I called and the agent there was very kind and helpful and moved very quickly on my behalf. A letter explaining my current situation was sent to the IRS along with five years of tax returns. Within one week, I received a call from the agent. He informed me that I had been removed from all collection activity and placed in a status called "Uncollectible." I would receive a letter once a year from the IRS showing what I owed, and would never be billed for it again, but, if I become financially able, I will have to repay it.

"I am called to wealth, so when I move into that financially able place, I will happily repay it!

"All of these blessings added up to about $75,000!

"God is so good. I can't thank Him enough!"

PRAYER FOR SUPERNATURAL SUPPLY

I choose to understand, comprehend, believe and receive the proclamation of the prophet:

I proclaim vast amounts of wealth to be released supernaturally. I unearth vast riches of hidden treasure. I call forth fresh, creative ways for you to gain wealth according to Deuteronomy 8:18.

I speak that God has spoken through His prophets that the wealth of the wicked must be released to the righteous. This is the Word of God.

"A good man leaves an inheritance to his children's children, but the wealth of the sinner is stored up for the righteous" (Proverbs 13:22 NKJV).

I proclaim to powers of darkness that the powers of light will flourish and you, devil, are defeated in the authority of the name of Jesus Christ.

Satan, you are old and ugly and defeated and the hole that you have dug for the people of God, we put you into it.

May the angel of the Lord pursue you on a dark and slippery path. And everything you have taken in time, talent, and treasure I command you to restore it seven times!

Father, I thank You right now that satan cannot obstruct the transfer of wealth. I activate the realms of the miraculous as we open every prison door and let every captive go free.

Lord God, I thank You that every evil power of darkness has been broken by the blood of Jesus, the Christ of God.

I take the apostolic and prophetic authority of God almighty which has been given to me and

I bind you mammon, you vile, disgusting spirit. You will not touch the chosen ones of God.

Father, I thank You for Your Word. I thank You that it has the power to inform and transform.

Father, thank You for each and every person reading these proclamations. We thank You for setting them free from the plans of the enemy.

Lord God, the steps of the righteous have been ordered by You, so we choose to follow You. We thank You, Lord God, that Christ in us is the hope of glory. Father, we thank You that through faith in Jesus Your power is being released. Amen

Beloved what I have just done is program you for greatness by the infallible Word of God. What I have just spoken over you is in alignment with the written Word of God.

We prophecy according to our faith. We proclaim according to the Word of God. And we begin to find out that the purpose of a real, true, prophetic word is that the prophetic voice of God has the power to inform and transform our lives when you and I choose to believe and receive the Word of God.

You and I already have
what it takes to rise
above the status quo.

5

Shifting Your Circumstances into a Position of Favor

Then God said, "Let there be light"; and there
was light. – Genesis 1:3 (NKJV)

From the very beginning when God Almighty proclaimed, "Let there be light," immediately there was
light. The will of God is always creative, and the Word of
God will activate the will of God. Paul imparted incredible wisdom and understanding to Timothy when he said,
'You must war. You must stand and not faint with the
things that belong to you.'

There will be words that will be proclaimed over your
life which are in conjunction with the infallible, inerrant,
and awesome Word of God. Those words are alive and you
cannot say, "Well, I'm just going to put those in the pantry

and we'll see if they'll come to pass." No, you have to say, "Thanks be to God who always causes me to triumph in every situation."

The words out of your mouth create an environment conducive for the Word of God to be consumed in the room of your heart. Then, out of the abundance of that heart, you open your mouth and create with the Word of God.

I read an article about proclamations that touched my heart and triggered my faith to see the worth of a proclamation. The article talked about Dr. N. Jerome Stowell, a prominent American scientist and confirmed atheist. While he was working in a large laboratory of a clinic, he had an incredible experience which caused him to change his mind.

Remember, we are talking about the secrets behind the power of proclaiming the Word of God. The Word of God has the power to perform itself.

Dr. Stowell was assigned the task of measuring the wavelength and force of the radiation of the human brain. He and his colleagues wanted to examine what occurs in the human brain while passing from life to death. Shortly before the death of a woman with terminal brain cancer, a highly sensitive recorder and microphone were placed beside her bed. The scientists waited in an adjoining side chamber. During the final moments before her death, she was heard praying and praising God. Her prayers and praise went as follows: She implored God to forgive all those who had wronged her during her life. Then she gave full expression of her faith in God by saying, "I know that You are and will remain the only reliable source of power for all Your creatures." She thanked Him for His strength with which He had supported her all her life and for the assurance that she belonged to Jesus. She proclaimed to Him that, in spite of all her suffering, her love for Him had not diminished. As she recalled the forgiveness of her sins through the blood of Jesus Christ, her words revealed an indescribable joy. Finally, she exulted in the joy and knowledge that she would soon see her Savior. Dr. Stowell and his colleagues were so moved that they openly wept, unashamed of their tears and completely forgetting what they had been assigned to do.

While the woman continued to pray, Dr. Stowell and his team heard a clicking sound from their instruments. They found the indicator to be at 500 degrees positive with the radiation energy exceeding the scale of their instruments. They had now, with the help of a technical survey, made a tremendous discovery; the brain of a dying woman who was in contact with God developed a power which was 55 times stronger than the output of a world-wide broadcast message.

In the reverse, and through continuing investigation, an irritated mentally insane man using the name of God in a blasphemous way and spewing forth insults and curses had the exact same effect on the instruments, except that the instruments went 500 degrees negative.

Through instrumental measurements they had established what occurs in the human brain while transgressing one of the Ten Commandments, and Dr. Stowell's atheistic philosophy of life began to crumble. He said, "Even I was standing before the omniscient God. The foolishness of my unbelief continued to become clearer to me. Since I wanted to be honest with myself, I could not close out the penetrating truth. Thus, I became a happy disciple of Jesus and learned to believe in Jesus Christ as my personal Savior."[3]

Job 22:28 says, "Decree a thing and it will be established unto you." Job's life was a disaster when he spoke those words. Even his wife told him to curse God and die. But he stood fast, proclaiming his faith and believing God. The Patriarchs and the great men and women of God knew the secret behind the power of proclaiming God's Word.

As you continue to read these pages, you will learn how to use your words and faith in God to literally shift the circumstances in your life into a position of favor. If you have been in a situation where your body needs healing, your circumstances need a breakthrough, or your finances

---

3 (Article by Dr. N. Jerome Stowell: http://www.the-new-way. org/testimonies/conv_varie_049_the_power_of_prayer.html)

need a miracle touch from God, begin by replacing unbelief with belief and a positive Word of God.

You and I, because we are born again and house God, already have what it takes to rise above the status quo. We are extraordinary creatures. The Word of God tells us that, at the time you believed and received Christ, confessed with your mouth and believed in your heart that Jesus Christ, the Son of God, is the one that has conquered hell, death and the grave, you became a living quickened spirit; a new creation. In the Greek language, a new creation actually means a heavenly species. You and I still look like we are humans, but this is only our earth suit and God, by the spirit of revelation, doing what only God can do, has turned us into a heavenly species.

Our purpose is to administrate the estate of God from the revelation of a finished work. It is there that we study how God rules and reigns. He does it with his mouth. We are learning that, "Unto him that orders his conversation righteous, will I show the salvation of God." Now the salvation of God offers the benefits of total healing, deliverance, peace, and prosperity.

If we want the benefit, let's learn about the procedure. Let's begin to find out what we are supposed to do to get ourselves in, or out, of situations by proclaiming the Word of God and seeing it established.

I remember distinctly when I knew nothing about supernatural healing. I just knew that I needed it. I had tuberculosis and asthma. Then I went to a Kathryn Kuhlman meeting and she proclaimed over me. She laid her beautiful hands on me and said, "Oh, Father, such as You have given me, I give it to her." I had no idea what that meant. I did not understand the purpose of impartation or proclamations. I just knew I was standing there in front of her and, when she laid her hands on me, I was thrown about 15 feet under Dino's piano in front of about three or 4,000 people and my life was dramatically changed by the words that were proclaimed.

The Old Testament word for "faith" is obedience, while the New Testament word means to pursue; to cross over. We are crossing over to possess what is ours; the land that flows with milk (the sincere Word of God) and honey (revelation). You are that land. I proclaim that you, the reader, are a land that flows with milk and honey. God has spoken through His Word that the wealth of the wicked must be released to the righteous.

Thank You, Lord God, that You are transforming and transferring the understanding that, as new creatures, we are the sons of God. We have a new bloodline, a new destiny, a new purpose, a new lineage, and a new life. You have taken away the old to establish the new. Father, thank You that there is a power being released.

We learn His Word, know His voice, and the voice of another we will not hear. We are among the blessed and chosen ones. One day I asked the Lord what constitutes 'many are called and few are chosen.' How do we become the chosen of God? He told me that the chosen ones are the ones who choose to believe.

> "For as the rain comes down, and the snow from heaven, And do not return there, But water the earth, And make it bring forth and bud, That it may give seed to the sower And bread to the eater, So shall My word be that goes forth from My mouth; It shall not return to Me void, But it shall accomplish what I please, And it shall prosper in the thing for which I sent it" (Isaiah 55:10-11, NKJV).

You and I are the launching pad for the Word of God which has the power to heal the sick, raise the dead, drive out demons, and preach good news. To be blessed means empowered to be wealthy; and wealthy does not mean money only, but that you are truly rich when you are filled with the desire to know and serve the living God.

The power of proclamations includes financial provision, financial independence, the releasing of wealth, and the sevenfold restoration of time and talent. The power of God's Word is able to put all of that back into place again in a way that was better than it ever was before.

The following testimony, by Linda, is a great demonstration of this truth.

Awakening Your God-Given Gifts

"Every good gift and every perfect gift is from above, and comes down from the Father of lights, with whom there is no variation or shadow of turning" (James 1:17 NKJV).

"After Dr. Clarice prayed for me, I prayed for a purpose. God opened a door for me to have a watercolor painting ministry. In eight weeks I painted 52 paintings. I sold 30 of them nationwide. I had an art show and sold 19. The best and greatest thing is that people know that it's God doing this and not me. It is an open door to share Jesus. Each painting has a cross they have to find like a treasure and a Bible verse. The most supernatural thing is that I didn't even know I could paint! People say they feel peace when they look at my paintings. I am blown away by God answering your prayer.

"Dr. Clarice prayed for me, 'I decree and declare that new doors of opportunity will arise, that you and your family will have no hesitation walking through them, and that they will be purpose and destiny filled.'

Her prayers were answered. I now have my own painting business which is called **JOY WORKS by Linda D.**

~I have painted 250 paintings in 12 weeks.

~They have sold all over the country.

~God's Word is in over 120 homes across the country.

~Each painting has a Bible verse and cross on it.

~I have been in three art shows and won the People's Choice Award.

~I have a speaking engagement to share my testimony.

~The paintings have been turned into fabric to make clothing and pillows.

This is nothing short of a miracle!

As of today's date, my painting business continues to flourish and I have now expanded into taking referrals to coach and mentor others who are interested in painting or starting a painting business.

You have the ability
to change the
atmosphere of the
earth as you send up
the Word of God.

6

The Power of Creating a Partnership between Your Words & Your Faith

W e have such an incredible opportunity to learn about God's Word and about the power of creating a partnership between our words and our faith. Be encouraged to know that the Word of God combined with a practical understanding of what happens when you align your words with His, makes you an unstoppable champion.

We find all the time that there are many people struggling with feelings of being overwhelmed, of inadequacy, stagnation, and hopelessness. It is not an unusual thing that, in this life, we are going to have some trials and tests. If you know in advance that those types of things are going to come, and that moods are going to swing in and out, keep in mind that the devil is just as active with his nasty lying mouth as he can be.

I am sure all of us have had times in our lives where we felt a little stuck, and somewhat overwhelmed. I am here to tell you that you do not have to stay that way. You can make a decision. A decision is not a conversion necessarily but, until you make a decision, until there is intention in your life to embrace change, everything in your life will stay the same.

This book is here to help you get unstuck, and then move into the manifestation of answered prayer.

Change Lives with Your Words

You have the ability to change the atmosphere of the earth as you send up the Word of God. As you proclaim the truth, which is the Word of God, believe that it will be established. When we see an individual bound by drugs, alcohol, wrong relationships, and other negative things, we have the ability to create a positive outcome with the fruit of our lips.

I once attended an event where the majority of the congregation were pastors and other men and women that were established in ministry. Toward the end of the meeting, I was giving away some products. I have a set of CDs called A Merry Heart. As I presented these CDs I spoke that, according to Scripture, a merry heart does good like medicine and told my audience that this set of CDs was a compilation of all kinds of funny stories that would make them laugh. I said, "If you've been oppressed, suppressed, repressed, or possessed, this is the set for you."

Way back in the furthest corner of the room was this little woman that got up and began to walk toward me. Her little shoulders were slumped over, her head was wrapped up in a rag, and her countenance was expressionless. It was obvious to me that she was very oppressed by great demonic spirits of addiction and suicide. This little lady was just eaten up with oppression.

I knew it was taking every ounce of energy that was in her to walk down that aisle. As she was getting closer to me, I began to proclaim, "I see this woman healed, delivered, and prosperous. I proclaim that she is a disciple taught of the Lord with great peace and undisturbed composure." By the time she got up to me, I ran to her, she ran to me, I threw my arms around her, and held her. I cried, she cried, everybody in the audience cried. It was not anything that had to be spoken. It was the compassion of Almighty God seeing no one except in Christ, simply creating with the fruit of my lips, and the fruit of my heart.

When I stepped back and looked at her face, it was radiant. By proclaiming the Word of God, she was completely delivered from the demonic force that had her locked up. I did not have to get clever, I just agreed with God and said what He said. I became a launching pad for His power to do warfare against those evil spirits.

Some time ago, I got the sweetest letter from a lady I had been mentoring. She wrote this:

"Dear Dr. Clarice, please let me thank you so much for the wonderful, truly magnificent proclamations that God gave to you and you spoke over us. I have already received extraordinary breakthrough in revelation far exceeding that which was before, which was truly groundbreaking even then.

Specifically, I want to add that, back in June before our sessions began, the Lord Himself by the Spirit of wisdom and revelation gave me Proverbs 13:22 to proclaim and many like scriptures. When your proclamation included the same scriptures, I just felt like the power of God came all over me and I began to declare in the name of the Lord Jesus that I received with great joy every word you had spoken over us.

Wow. Wow. Wow. Yes, the Lord has been bringing me through much that goes against those things traditionally that in the past I've understood. He is truly breaking off of me all man-made traditions and thinking and is causing me to stand on only the truth of His Word. I will proclaim the truth."

I have received several pieces of correspondence, all saying that their life has been not just challenged, but changed by proclamations spoken over them. Revelation which cannot be earned or learned only comes by the quickening voice of the Holy Spirit.

Embrace the Benefit. Embrace the Procedure.

Everything I am teaching you here is in perfect alignment with the Word of God; but, like all things, until they become yours by the reason of use, knowledge of a thing is not necessarily possession of it. If you want the benefit of an effective prayer life, then you have to embrace the way. The benefit is one thing, the procedure is another.

I have said many times, "Oh, I would love to play the piano." What I am actually saying is that I would love to sit down and have the benefit, but I would not love to submit to the discipline that would be required to do it. You need to have passion in order to have the performance that is going to set you aside as an unstoppable champion.

Know Who You Are

Scripture says, 'The righteous are as bold as a lion, and those who know God will do exploits.'

It is important to come to the place where you say, "I have to look and understand that champions live differently than ordinary people" regardless of whether or not you feel like a champion. My advice to you is, change your mind because you are a child of the most high God. You are not ordinary, you are now extraordinary.

You might look the same way you did before you got saved, but according to the infallible, inerrant awesome Word of God, you are not that same person. God, by His sovereignty, has birthed you to be a champion. Scripture tells us to allow, or let this mind that is in Christ, dwell in you richly. The carnal mind is enmity with God. It cannot comprehend, or understand; therefore, it will never agree. You have to put carnal thinking down and choose to exercise yourself unto godliness.

You have to develop the power of having a proclamation so that your thought life comes under the discipline of the Holy Spirit. You will find that the most significant and important thing any of us have is a thought because, what we think is ultimately what we are going to say, and what we say is what we are going to do. That is the way it works. Thought, word, action.

Knowing who you are in Christ is imperative before you begin to make proclamations. I hear people say, "I'm fat, I'm old, I forgot I can't do what I used to do. I have this, or that, wrong with me. I'm unhappy. I find fault with everything. This isn't good. That's not good." Saying those things about yourself is actually releasing a negative spirit.

Reflect Like a Pearl

We have said before that, when you proclaim this over yourself, something incredible happens in your brain when your ears hear the frequency and the vibration of your voice. Remember, just like you have a fingerprint, you also have a voice print. You have a DNA that is unique to you. God deposited something of Himself into you that no other living creature ever has, or ever will have. God has sent Himself throughout the face of the earth in His body so that you and I absorb and reflect like a pearl.

A pearl is the only gem that has the ability to absorb and reflect. That is why the scripture sometimes refers to the kingdom of Heaven being like a merchant. Jesus goes out and sells everything He has to purchase the pearl of great price. It is imperative to understand that, if you are going to be looking for pearls, you have to go into the sea, the sea of humanity, and there you find pearls in oysters.

Unfortunately, every oyster does not produce a pearl. Only those that have spent their existence being irritated will become pearls. Their suffering has formed a substance inside of them that makes them precious. Do not waste your suffering, and your sorrow, because the merchant man, which is Jesus, says, 'In the light of the glory that is to be revealed, the suffering is not to be considered.'

Whatever you hear the most is what you are going to have faith in.

If you are proclaiming over yourself, "I am a head, and not the tail. I am above, and not beneath. I am blessed. I am empowered. I am the righteousness of God. My life is hidden in Christ. It is no longer I, but now it is Christ," those words have to be said over and over until the brain gets a hold of it. Instead of it being just a little line going through your brain, now you have formed a groove in your brain, like building a ditch, or a channel, where those words hit a critical mass and the information becomes revelation. They go down into your heart where your spirit, soul, and body can agree. That information becomes transformation, through revelation, and then, out of the abundance of your heart, your mouth proclaims.

Whatever those words are that you say about yourself, your spouse, your government, your president, are either building momentum for positive, or negative. It is a decision. A decision is never a conversion, but until you make a decision, then and only then when you act upon what you say will there come an incredible ability, the witness of the spirit, to change the atmosphere.

All Power in Heaven and in Earth Has Been Given to You

The scripture says, 'Know you not that the angels are ministering spirits sent forth from God to help us who are the heirs of salvation?' You and I do not have the power to order angels around, but what angels do respond to is the proclaimed Word of God and they say to each other, 'I hear the children of God saying they are healed, delivered, prosperous, and that their children are disciples taught of the Lord. They are proclaiming this. Go watch over their words to perform it. Bless them coming in, and bless them going out.' The Word of God says that all power in heaven and in earth has been given to the church.

The Power of a Negative Attitude

An individual can enter a room with a negative attitude and change the very atmosphere of that room, or party, or wherever it is. When they carry gloom, doom, frustration, and judgment, it is like a stench that has the power to change everything negatively. It has the power to summon demonic forces because it is filled with unbelief. Without faith, it is impossible to please God.

When people begin to say negative things like, "My children are ruined. My children are in jail. My husband is a failure. My wife is this, or that," there is a literal alarm that goes off in hell. Demon forces say, "We smell unbelief.

81

The children of God say their children are failures. They say that they are sick, oppressed, and lonely. They are confessing the negative instead of professing and proclaiming the positive." Remember, life and death are in your mouth.

You are an unstoppable, incredible agent of goodness. You can proclaim a thing, and it will be established. There is an energy that this creates around you. I like to call it a magnetic force so that when you tell people you are a money magnet, a joy magnet, a light magnet, these are what you will draw to yourself. What you honor, you draw to yourself. It is just a fact.

You Can Either Heal or Kill with the Words You Speak

I have found that what you focus on is where the anointing flows. If you are focusing on positive things, on the Word of God, then your proclamations are actually establishing the Kingdom of God. Let your words be filled with love and light and understand that you can either heal, or kill, with the words that you speak.

When I was a little girl about five years old, my Aunt Mildred, who was such an authority figure, was about six feet tall. When you are five years old, somebody who is six feet tall can be very imposing even though she was actually as sweet as she could be. One day when she was talking to my mother, she turned to her and said, "Clarice has that olive skin." Well, the only olive I had ever seen was green.

Her words came from a place of authority and, because I was immature and did not know any better, I went and looked in the mirror, and wondered if people really thought I was green, or if there was something wrong with me. It caused all kinds of insecurity. One little simple thing from a person that has authority can cause all kinds of confusion. You begin to realize there are people you have, and will continue to come in contact with, who are speaking words over you without realizing that they are actually making a proclamation. When you do the same thing and are not careful with your words, you may actually say things that will cripple or hurt them rather than lift them up.

I had to grow up and get healed of thinking I was an olive. You may think that is funny, but when people you recognize as authority figures, such as teachers, parents, grandparents, uncles, and aunts, have carelessly said things, and proclaimed something over you, it can stultify your growth.

In the authority of the name of Jesus, I speak the blessings of God to you. I speak to those words that have been spoken over you and I say that they are going to begin to create a partnership between your faith, the love of God, and the proclamations that you are going to make over yourself, and others. You are moving on from the limitations and going to see yourselves, from now on, as unstoppable champions. You will proclaim a thing, it will be positive, it will be according to the Word of God, and it is going to be established for you.

Take these words that I am speaking to you, apply them, and begin to proclaim over yourself.

7

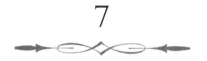

Hearing God's Voice

Who would agree with God that greater is He that is in you than he that is in the world?

According to the Word of God, Colossians 2:10 promises that I am complete in Him who is the head. I am alive with Christ. I am free from the law of sin and death. I am free from all oppression and fear.

I have the Greater One living inside of me because greater is He that is in me than he that is in the world. We have received the gift of righteousness. By Himself He paid the price for low self-esteem, unworthiness, all of these lies that the enemy tries to sow as corruptible weed into our garden.

It may not look glorious, but the Word of God says the earth is filled with the knowledge of the glory of the Lord. We are the earth that is filled with the knowledge of the glory of the Lord. It is our time to arise and shine for the light has come for the glory of God.

I have no lack. I have no need. I am not sick, oppressed, lonely, or depressed. I am not blood cursed. I am blood blessed. We who stand in the blood of the Lamb of God who takes away all the sins of the world arise as mighty warriors. You are mighty men and women who proclaim the following:

> Regardless of what has been assigned against me, my great faith in the Word of God says that no trial or test has come upon me that God has not already given me the ability to make 100% on because I am going in on His test strength, not my own. God has already done it for me.

When we tell ourselves that we do not know how we are going to pay a certain bill, and the doctor says we are going down, and our kids also need money, we have begun to listen to the accuser. We have begun to listen to his lies. If I look at facts, I will turn into one, but if I look at truth, that is what I become because the Word of God says we are changed from glory to glory into that which we are looking at. We become that which we adore.

The Word of God tells us in Hebrews 1:7 that the angels are ministering spirits. God sends those angelic beings that respond to the Word of God when you speak the Word of God in faith, and in love.

Early in my ministry I was teaching people that a believer can have what they say if it is scriptural. That is what the Bible teaches us. I believed that the reason they did not have enough money was because they kept talking about how poor they were. When you say you cannot afford this or that, cannot buy good toilet paper, and cannot have the luxuries of life, you begin to think poor all the time. I remember the time in my own life when I had no money, and five hungry kids. I asked, "Lord, why are You putting me through this?" And He asked, "What do you want?"

I said, "Lord, it's obvious what I want. I want some food, a car, and some money." He said, "Well, go to the grocery store and get your groceries." So, I put my hair up in a ponytail, had no makeup on because, if I was poor, I wanted to look poor. And then I said, "Lord, I don't have a way to get to the store."

I do not know if any of you have been poor like me. I did not like it then, and do not like it now. Poverty is my number one enemy.

God said, "Get dressed nicely and look like a child of the King. Look like royalty." I had a fur coat that I had tried to sell for $5.00 to buy hamburger meat but they thought I had stolen it so they wouldn't buy it from me. I put that same fur coat on and looked like I was up to something special. I simply sat in my kitchen and waited, and after about 30 minutes my friend came by and asked me where I was going all dressed up.

At first, I said, "I'm going to buy groceries." Then I said, "No, I'm going to get groceries." She asked, "Do you have some money?" Everybody knew I was broke. I said, "I didn't tell you I had any money. I'm just telling you God told me to go get the groceries." She asked, "Are you going to steal them?" I said, "No, I'm just obeying God."

And so, she drove me to the store and I filled my grocery cart. I remembered reading about Pat Robertson when he was going through a real hard time and was going to exist on soy beans. Well, that never happened to me. I just never wanted soy beans. I took one grocery cart, then a second one, got steak, and still did not know who was going to pay for it. I had both grocery carts packed when my friend said, "Look, I've got $50.00 and that won't even cover one grocery cart so I'll help you put all of this back." Be careful who your friends are. I pushed both grocery carts right up to the cash register fully expecting God to pay the bill.

I got checked through with the first cart and started on the second when an attorney from our town walked up with a chicken and loaf of bread in his hand. He said, "Well, well. Look at the affluent, Miss Fluitt." I asked, "How are you today, James?" He responded with, "I just wish I could hear from God the way you and your husband say that you do. I wish God would just speak to me." I said, "Why don't you quit wishing and just begin to say, "God, speak to me?"" He laughed and jokingly said, "God, please speak to me." Then, he looked at me and exclaimed, "Oh, no!" I said, "What's the matter?" He replied, "God spoke to me. I heard God speak." I said, "Great." He said, "Terrible. God told me to buy all of your groceries."

Dear reader, you do not get stories like this if you do not move out in faith. I believe God is waiting for us to understand that He is watching over every word which comes out of your mouth. Life and death are in your tongue.

I want to proclaim over your money but first, remember when I told the people, "Your problem is that you talk poor, think poor, and out of the abundance of your heart your words testify against God? You say you can't have a car, can't have a house, don't have a job, your Social Security didn't come in, you're just a poor, pitiful mess." What kind of talk is that? Your words are killing you.

One day this lady brought me a little black toy Pomeranian puppy. I took the little thing home and my husband said, "Where'd you get the dog?" I replied, "Well, I was teaching about people who need to get a dog and name him money. Somebody gave me a dog and called it Money." He said, "Honey, you cannot call that dog Money." I asked, "Why?" He said, "Well, people will misunderstand you." I responded with, "You're a little late in the game over here. I'm already misunderstood." So, we kept the dog and I would say, "Money, come here. Money, rollover. Money, deposit. Money, stay."

I learned how to talk to my sweet Money, then we got Money a puppy friend and named her Debt Free!

Now I would like to proclaim over your money.

Father, in the authority of the name of Jesus, we open the portals of heaven for avenues of revenue. We thank You for the ingenuity that is released to start all kinds of businesses. Thank You that doing business according to the Word of God is honorable. We are going to stop confessing poverty and begin to thank You that Your Word says You would, above everything, that we prosper and be in health even as our soul prospers. When our soul begins to agree with our spirit, we will see the benefits of the richness of God manifest in our lives. And all the people said, amen.

8

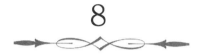

The Power and Purpose of Proclamations

Thanks be to God who always, every time, causes me to triumph. Before there is release, pull back your spiritual bow and let your arrows flow. You will never possess what you are not willing to pursue. There will be a lot of tension in your life because tension and release is the story of life.

Now learn and be aware that you house destiny. Do not allow yourself to grow weary in doing good, for when fatigue walks in, faith walks out and unbelief builds a nest in your soul.

Beloved, lay your hands on yourself right now and proclaim:

Father, in Jesus' name, I proclaim that I am who You say that I am. I command fatigue, weariness, frustration, laziness, impropriety, and obesity, to loose me. I am not sick, oppressed, lonely, or poor. I thank You, Lord, that You are my provider and I will not just exist from day to day. I open my heart and believe what You say.

Everything that You did not tell me to do I command to be set free from. I have focus, vision, perception, and discernment. I carry the antidote to every negative situation. I refuse to look back thinking about defeat.

This is the day that You have made. Every seed that You did not plant, I am plucking out. I command depression to leave me. I refuse to spend my money, energy, or time on anything that You did not originate.

I am a candidate for the realm of the miraculous. Hear me, O God, as I proclaim that these bones shall live again.

It's time to fly like an eagle.

Proclaim with Me!

I proclaim that
each reader and
their family is filled
with the distinctive
nature of God.

9

God's Character

"The Lord is not slack concerning His promise, as some count slackness, but is longsuffering toward us, not willing that any should perish but that all should come to repentance" (2 Peter 3:9 NKJV).

"Every good gift and every perfect gift is from above, and comes down from the Father of lights, with whom there is no variation or shadow of turning" (James 1:17 NKJV).

I proclaim that each reader and their family is filled with the distinctive nature of God.

PROCLAMATIONS

Today, I choose to agree with God! I proclaim my life is an example of God's extravagance. He always performs far above anything I could ask, think, or imagine. He is an "above and beyond" God.

95

Today, I choose to agree with God! The Lord God awakens me every morning to fellowship with Him, and He opens my ears to hear what His spirit is speaking to me.

Today, I choose to agree with God! I am always acknowledging the Lord in all my ways and He is always directing my steps. He is such a wonderful God!

10

Character and Fruit of the Spirit

"Finally, brethren, whatever things are true, whatever things are noble, whatever things are just, whatever things are pure, whatever things are lovely, whatever things are of good report, if there is any virtue and if there is anything praiseworthy—meditate on these things" (Philippians 4:8 NKJV).

"But the fruit of the Spirit is love, joy, peace, longsuffering, kindness, goodness, faithfulness" (Galatians 5:22 NKJV).

PROCLAMATIONS

Today, I choose to agree with God! The love, peace, and hope of God is more and more evident in and through me every day.

Today, I choose to agree with God! I have spent time with the lover of my soul and I am fully able to love people really, really well.

Today, I choose to agree with God! I am filled with the joy of the Lord, and people are happy to be around me.

Today, I choose to agree with God! I love and honor all people. I respond to people in kindness and love.

Today, I choose to agree with God! I am not afraid, but I am confident in God. I have perfect love in my heart, and perfect love pushes out fear.

Today, I choose to agree with God! I choose to let the peace of Christ rule in my heart. As a member of one body, I am called to peace and I am thankful for the safety I have in God.

Today, I choose to agree with God! I walk in a manner worthy of the Lord, pleasing Him in all respects. I bear fruit in every good work and I am increasing in the knowledge of God.

Today, I choose to agree with God! I proclaim I am filled with the fullness of God's love. I am able to pour love out to others because God has poured His love into me.

Today, I choose to agree with God! I will walk in strong character and integrity. I will stand firm in God's promises with clarity.

Today, I choose to agree with God! The joy of the Lord is my strength. I can joyfully and confidently accomplish anything that He sets before me.

Today, I choose to agree with God! God's love is being made perfect in me. I choose to walk in love and honor to those I encounter today, and every day.

Today, I choose to agree with God! I proclaim that I have eyes to see. I see people through the eyes of God and not from my own understanding.

Today, I choose to agree with God! I proclaim that I walk in integrity and with honor. I respect those around me, and those around me respect me. I bear good fruit in everything I do, and I am increasing in the knowledge of God.

Today, I choose to agree with God! I see people through the eyes of God. I see each and every person, not according to their current state, but according to their full potential.

Today, I choose to agree with God! I choose to trust in Him and walk in forgiveness.

Today, I will walk in
new authority because
He makes all things
new.

11

Attitudes, Beliefs, Mindsets, and Perspectives

The most important thing you have is a God-inspired Word that produces a God-inspired attitude which releases a God-empowered mindset and perspective.

"I will praise You for I am fearfully and wonderfully made; Marvelous are Your works, And that my soul knows very well" (Psalm 139:14 NKJV).

PROCLAMATIONS

Today, I choose to agree with God! I wear happy really good. I am full of God's joy and I am a delight to be around.

Today, I choose to agree with God! I will not fear what life may bring my way because I know that His mercies are new each and every day.

Today, I choose to agree with God! This is a new day! A day of hope. A day of blessings. A day of favor. A day of freedom and forgiveness. Today, I will walk in new authority because He makes all things new.

Today, I choose to agree with God! Every day is a good day. Today is the day that the Lord has made, and today is that day.

Today, I choose to agree with God! My mind is expanding, and my way of thinking is growing. My mind is a powerful gift from God.

Today, I choose to agree with God! I proclaim that my mind is alert, and my heart is open to God. I make right decisions that move me closer to my defined destiny. Today, I will agree with God.

Today, I choose to agree with God! I will face today with confidence in who I am and whose I am. I will boldly walk in the direction of my dreams and goals with a positive mindset and attitude.

Today, I choose to agree with God! I proclaim, I am God's masterpiece. He created me with great purpose. God has a beautiful plan already established.

Today, I choose to agree with God! I have the wisdom of God. I make right choices and I do the right things. I follow the direction of God and see success in my life.

Today, I choose to agree with God! I proclaim I will think and be positive. I will establish my plans and work toward fulfilling them.

Today, I choose to agree with God! I hear the voice of the Lord. I will follow where He leads me. I will do what He asks me to do. I always do the right thing, in the right way, at the right time.

Today, I choose to agree with God! I proclaim my life is an example of God's extravagance. He always performs far above anything I could ask, think, or imagine. He is an "above and beyond" God!

Today, I choose to agree with God! This is the day the Lord has made. I will rejoice and be glad in it.

Today, I choose to agree with God! I will have a positive outlook on life. No matter what things look like on the outside, I will choose to see life, hope, and peace in every situation.

Today, I choose to agree with God! I am happy. I am healthy. I am strong. God's plan for my life is good. When I follow Him, I can't go wrong.

Today, I choose to agree with God! No matter what things look like, I have made up my mind, I will always look on the bright side.

Today, I choose to agree with God! I was created to shine and stand out. The opinions and thoughts of others will not keep me down. God made me to stand tall, and to shine bright. And, I will do just that.

Today, I choose to agree with God! This is a day of celebration. I choose to be positive and grateful for all of my blessings.

Today, I choose to agree with God! This is the day God has made. I choose to be happy and celebrate today.

Today, I choose to agree with God! My mind is alert and sharp. I make fast, accurate, and great decisions. God's blessing is on my life.

Today, I choose to agree with God! When life hands me lemons, I will learn to make lemonade. I choose to stay positive in all things, and in all ways.

Today, I choose to agree with God! I will keep a positive attitude in all I do. When things do not go the way that they should, I just keep on smiling and say, God is good!

Today, I choose to agree with God! I proclaim that I am empowered to jump over obstacles and win the race.

Today, I choose to agree with God! I proclaim that I am a champion and I do not respond as normal people do. I respond like a winner.

Today, I choose to agree with God! I do not walk in fear. I am strong and courageous. I have peace, love, and a sound mind.

Today, I choose to agree with God. I am no longer limited by old mindsets and beliefs. I stand on the truth, and proclaim that I have been rescued and set free.

New doors of
opportunity are
opening, and new
breakthrough is
coming.

12

Family

From Genesis to Revelation you will discover that God's unit of measure for salvation is your household. You can create with your words of faith and call your family and friends to salvation.

"But as for me and my house, we will serve the Lord" (Joshua 24:15 NKJV).

"If it is possible, as much as depends on you, live peaceably with all men" (Romans 12:18 NKJV).

PROCLAMATIONS

Today, I choose to agree with God! I am safe and protected. God watches over me and my family. His angel armies shield me from my enemies.

Today, I choose to agree with God! I proclaim my family is safe and protected by angelic forces. There is nothing that can stop God's plan for our lives.

Today, I choose to agree with God! My children are blessed, and success is their future. God's love covers them with a good and happy life.

Today, I choose to agree with God! My children will fulfill their purpose and walk in the fullness of all God has for them.

Today, I choose to agree with God! I proclaim my children walk in divine relationships. They have the favor of God in all areas of their life.

Today, I choose to agree with God! My family is safe and protected. The heavenly hosts stand watch and guard over my family each and every day.

Today, I choose to agree with God! I proclaim supernatural provision and the divine manifestation of miracles in my family. Things that have been blocked are now being released.

Today, I choose to agree with God! I proclaim promotion and elevation over my family. I proclaim new doors of opportunity are opening, and new breakthrough is coming.

Today, I choose to agree with God! I proclaim there is greatness in my DNA. My generational lines are blessed, and inheritance flows to me and my family.

Today, I choose to agree with God! I proclaim my family will agree with God. My children and my grandchildren are safe, protected, and walking in the divine favor of God.

Today, I choose to agree with God! I proclaim that God's love flows freely through me. I meditate on things above, and blessings overflow to my family.

Today, I choose to agree with God! I proclaim that my children are safe and secure. I proclaim they are protected and shielded from harm. Today, supernatural favor and love surround them wherever they go.

Today, I choose to agree with God! My family is blessed and protected. My generations are favored of God. I receive the fullness of my inheritance in God.

Today, I choose to agree with God! My family walks in peace and love. My children are highly skilled and very talented. Their gifts make room for them to succeed.

Today, I choose to agree with God! I will speak life and blessings to others. My family is blessed and prosperous.

Today, I choose to agree with God! I will speak life to my family and my circumstance. I have the power to bring life to dead situations.

13

Relationships

I have decided that, to have successful relationships, I must be kind, merciful, and forgiving toward myself and others.

> "And above all things have fervent love for one another, for "love will cover a multitude of sins" (1 Peter 4:8 NKJV).

> "I, therefore, the prisoner of the Lord, beseech you to walk worthy of the calling with which you were called, with all lowliness and gentleness, with long-suffering, bearing with one another in love, endeavoring to keep the unity of the Spirit in the bond of peace" (Ephesians 4:1-3 NKJV).

Be yourself and others will respond with equal authenticity. This is the secret to building relationships. Be genuine and choose to spend time with those that respond in like manner.

I have developed a time-proven skill on how to be authentic, attentive and sensitive with those that I meet. It is simple; just be nice, smile, and express a sincere interest in others.

PROCLAMATIONS

Today, I choose to agree with God! I walk in grace and mercy in my relationships. I love and accept people exactly as they are.

Today, I choose to agree with God! I proclaim that God is sending new relationships my way. He is connecting me with covenant people.

Today, I choose to agree with God! I am considerate of others. I look out, not only for my own interests, but also for the interest of others.

Today, I choose to agree with God! I will be kind to other people. I have a tender heart and see others through the eyes of love and compassion.

Today, I choose to agree with God! I will look for opportunities to help those around me. When I see a need, I will be mobilized to serve. As I learn to serve, I learn to lead with the Lord's heart.

Today, I choose to agree with God! I will walk in love and be kind to those I encounter. I will smile big and share a warm greeting as my life becomes an outreach of God's love to those I meet.

Today, I choose to agree with God! I am kind and loving toward other people. God has positioned me to be a light to those around me. I am a carrier of God's love and peace.

Don't allow
circumstances to
control your emotions.

14

Health and Protection

Do you agree that, above all things, God's will is for you to be healthy and prosperous to the degree that your soul (intellect, reason, and emotions) agrees with God?

"Beloved, I pray that you may prosper in all things and be in health, just as your soul prospers" (3 John 1:2 NKJV).

Keys for Prospering Your Soul

Gods wants us to prosper in every area of our lives:

- Families
- Relationships
- Career
- Finances
- Attitude
- Physical body

The truth of God's Word is what will cause our soul to prosper (3 John 1:3-4).

"Now may the God of peace Himself sanctify you completely; and may your whole spirit, soul, and body be preserved blameless at the coming of our Lord Jesus Christ" (1 Thessalonians 5:23).

How do we get the four parts of your soul; your mind, will, intellect and emotions to prosper?

Mind - Get your mind into the realm of prosperity by renewing it daily through the washing of the Word of God by reading and meditating on it. **Romans 12:1-2**

Will - By aligning it with the will of God. With joy, submit your will to God's will. You will know His will by reading the inspired, inerrant Word of God.

Intellect - Hosea 4:6 – *My people perish for a lack of knowledge...* We gain knowledge by reading God's Word.

Emotions - Our emotions need to be balanced. Don't allow circumstances to control your emotions. Don't let them rule your life. Maintain self-control in all areas of your life. **Galatians 5:22-23**

PROCLAMATIONS

Today, I choose to agree with God! The Great Physician lives in me! I constantly have healing power flowing in and through me.

Today, I choose to agree with God! I am healed and set free from sickness and disease. My body is healthy and whole.

Today, I choose to agree with God! God sends His Word out and it protects, heals, and watches over me all the days of my life.

Today, I choose to agree with God! I am victorious and protected by the hand of God. I do not have to worry because the Lord causes my enemies to be scattered. Those who contend with me, God will contend with.

Today, I choose to agree with God! I walk in divine health and healing. The DNA of the creator flows in my veins. I make wise choices that benefit my body.

Today, I choose to agree with God! I proclaim I am strong and courageous. No weapon formed against me will stand. I am victorious against my enemies. God is on my side and fights on my behalf.

Today, I choose to agree with God! I am healed, healthy, whole, and thriving in every area of my life.

Today, I choose to agree with God! The very life of Jesus Christ is in me. I have great hearing and seeing naturally and supernaturally.

15

Identity

If any person is born again through faith in Jesus Christ, they have become a new creation, a heavenly species, a forgiven child of God. When God looks at the redeemed, He filters them through the blood of Jesus and all He sees is His Son.

> "Therefore, if anyone is in Christ, he is a new creation; old things have passed away; behold, all things have become new" (2 Corinthians 5:17 NKJV).

> "But you are a chosen generation, a royal priesthood, a holy nation, His own special people, that you may proclaim the praises of Him who called you out of darkness into His marvelous light" (1 Peter 2:9 NKJV).

Your identity is not something to be lost or trampled on. It is unique, special, and individualized to you and you alone! Know who you are and that you were created to be a success. You are here to make a difference in this world. Choose the things that will be beneficial in bringing you to your ultimate destination. You are a gift from God!

PROCLAMATIONS

Today, I choose to agree with God! Jesus takes great delight in me! He sings, rejoices, and dances over me.

Today, I choose to agree with God! I have the mind of Christ, and am thinking more and more like Him.

Today, I choose to agree with God! This day I will be everything God created me to be. I will be awesome, amazing, spectacular, delightful, happy, and free!

Today, I choose to agree with God! I have a relationship with Truth Himself and I am forever becoming more and more free.

Today, I choose to agree with God! I am a beautiful expression of the One that created me in His image and likeness.

Today, I choose to agree with God! I am handpicked by the King of the Universe! The Lord has chosen me for Himself, and I am His special treasure.

Today, I choose to agree with God! I have been made free in Christ. I am no longer a slave to sin. I am walking in my new identity as a child of the Most High.

Today, I choose to agree with God! I have been forgiven and set free. God's mercy covers me every morning. This is a new day, and I have new mercies today in my life.

PROCLAMATIONS

Today, I choose to agree with God! I have power, love, and a sound mind. I have erased fear from my life. I walk in the truth always. I know who I am in God.

Today, I choose to agree with God! I am being strengthened with power and might. I have great endurance and patience. I believe God's plan for my life.

Today, I choose to agree with God! I have divine access to God. The Word of God is clear to me. I have the ability to come boldly before God and make divine intercession.

Today, I choose to agree with God! I walk with intention. I intend to walk in righteousness. I intend to believe. I declare I am intentionally the righteousness of God.

Today, I will agree with God! I proclaim that I walk in perfect peace. God Himself is my peace. He fights my battles and rises to my defense. I have no cause for fear.

Today, I choose to agree with God! I am bold, strong, and courageous. God has not given me a spirit of fear. He gives me power, love, and self-discipline.

Today, I choose to agree with God! I am God's beloved child. He loves me exactly the way I am. I do not have to perform to earn His love. I just have to receive it.

Today, I choose to agree with God! I will speak with truth and honesty. I will uphold the standards of love, and walk with confidence freely.

Today, I choose to agree with God! His Word about me is true. God loves me and has great plans for my life. I will receive His love in my life today.

Today, I choose to agree with God! I will stand in the truth of who God says I am. I will not be swayed by the thoughts and opinions of others. The Lord is my defender and the lifter of my head.

Today, I choose to agree with God! I am fearfully and wonderfully made. God's love for me is great. I walk with integrity, and work with excellence. Favor is my companion.

Today, I choose to agree with God! I am victorious! Today, I will believe that no matter what I am going through, God is with me and He is fighting for me.

Today, I choose to agree with God! I am blessed and not stressed. I am appointed and not disappointed.

Today, I choose to agree with God! I am fearfully and wonderfully made. God loves me and goes before me to prepare the way for me.

Today, I choose to agree with God! I am a carrier of the Word of God. I carry love, joy, peace, and kindness. I convey the righteousness and truth of God.

Today, I choose to agree with God! Happiness, peace, and joy are mine. I walk each day with God by my side.

Today, I choose to agree with God! I have a relationship with the One that has solutions for every problem.

Today, I choose to agree with God! With Jesus, I always have hope to tap into.

Today, I choose to agree with God! There is not anything that God cannot do through me when I am fully aligned with Him.

Today, I choose to agree with God! I pursue love and prophesy everywhere that I go.

Today, I choose to agree with God! I have confidence in God. I walk by faith and not by sight.

Today, I choose to agree with God! My God chooses to dwell in temples not made with hands, and He has gladly made His home in me.

Today, I choose to agree with God! I am a worshiper. I wake up praising the Lord. I draw near to God and He draws near to me.

Today, I choose to agree with God! I have the mind of Christ. I think the thoughts of God.

Today, I choose to agree with God! I carry and express the beauty and gladness of God really well.

Today, I choose to agree with God! God doesn't just love me but likes and takes delight in me.

It is in your moment of
decision that destiny
is shaped.

16

My destiny is determined by my choices. My destiny can change with my choices, my purpose never changes.

Every action is parented by a decision. Before you can have an action, you have to make a decision. No matter how inconsequential it may seem, the smallest decision can literally change the outcome of your life. It is in your moment of decision that destiny is shaped.

"The Spirit of the Lord God is upon Me, Because the Lord has anointed Me To preach good tidings to the poor; He has sent Me to heal the broken-hearted, To proclaim liberty to the captives, And the opening of the prison to those who are bound; To proclaim the acceptable year of the Lord, And the day of vengeance of our God; To comfort all who mourn, To console those who mourn in Zion, To give them beauty for ashes, The oil of joy for mourning, The garment of praise for the spirit of heaviness; That they may be called trees of righteousness, The planting of the Lord, that He may be glorified" (Isaiah 61: 1-3 NKJV).

"Thou art worthy, O Lord, to receive glory and honor and power: for thou hast created all things, and thy pleasure they are and were created" (Revelation 4:11 KJV).

PROCLAMATIONS

Today, I choose to agree with God! I proclaim that I have a destiny and purpose. God has wonderful plans and expectations for my life.

Today, I choose to agree with God! I am a person of choice. I am presented with choices to make each day. I always choose correctly. I choose the righteous and life-giving plan of God.

Today, I choose to agree with God! I will lay down my plans and my expectations to embrace the plans and purposes of Heaven.

Today, I choose to agree with God! God is working in my life and on my behalf. He has some amazing things in store for me. I trust in Him as the future unfolds.

Today, I choose to agree with God! I do not have to worry about which way I will go. God has already prepared the way; so, today I will just go with the flow.

Today, I choose to agree with God! I walk in freedom. I embrace destiny. I live a full and happy life.

Today, I choose to agree with God! I am healed, thrilled, and filled. Nothing can stop me. I am pursuing love, chasing truth, and fulfilling my destiny.

Today, I choose to agree with God! I work from a place of rest and grace. My work is wonderful and successful!

The season of
increase is now.

17

Favor and Increase

"For You, O Lord, will bless the righteous; With favor You will surround him as with a shield" (Psalm 5:12 NKJV).

"May the Lord God of your fathers make you a thousand times more numerous than you are, and bless you as He has promised you" (Deuteronomy 1:11 NKJV).

"And his master saw that the Lord was with him and that the Lord made all he did to prosper in his hand. So Joseph found favor in his sight, and served him. Then he made him overseer of his house, and all that he had he put under his authority. So it was, from the time that he had made him overseer of his house and all that he had, that the Lord blessed the Egyptian's house for Joseph's sake; and the blessing of the Lord was on all that he had in the house and in the field" (Genesis 39:3-5 NKJV).

Increase is to make greater in size, amount, intensity, or degree; growing or making larger. The season of increase is now.

PROCLAMATIONS

Today, I choose to agree with God! I am blessed and favored. God goes before me and prepares the way. He watches over His words to see that they are fulfilled.

Today, I choose to agree with God! I am too blessed to be stressed, and I am too anointed to be disappointed. God holds my future, and everything is going to work out in my favor.

Today, I choose to agree with God! I proclaim answers are coming right away. It is the Word of the great Yahweh! Now, I can have whatever I pray.

Today, I choose to agree with God! I am showered with favor and increase in all areas of my life. God's blessings are all over me.

Today, I choose to agree with God! God prefers me and favors me wherever I go. I have been entrusted with the secrets of God. I am healthy, wealthy, and wise.

Today, I choose to agree with God! I have favor with God and man. Everything I put my hand to is blessed and prospers. I am anointed for success.

Today, I choose to agree with God! Good things overtake me in my life. Goodness and mercy follow me. I will love the Lord and live in His house forever.

Today, I choose to agree with God! I am going from grace to grace, strength to strength, and glory to glory.

Today, I choose to agree with God! I am alive and thriving! I believe in Jesus, and rivers of living waters flow from my innermost being.

Today, I choose to agree with God! My youth is being renewed daily. My strength is growing, and my faith is steadfast and sure.

Today, I choose to agree with God! I am being strengthened with all power according to His might! I have great endurance and patience. I can do all things through Christ who strengthens me.

Today, I choose to agree with God! This is a day of breakthrough. I have walked through the fire, and I have come out on the other side! My new season is here, TODAY.

I am designed to
live a successful,
abundant, and
prosperous life.

18

Success

"This Book of the Law shall not depart from your mouth, but you shall meditate in it day and night, that you may observe to do according to all that is written in it. For then you will make your way prosperous, and then you will have good success" (Joshua 1:8 NKJV).

"For I know the thoughts that I think toward you, says the LORD, thoughts of peace and not of evil, to give you a future and a hope" (Jeremiah 29:11 NKJV).

PROCLAMATIONS

Today, I choose to agree with God! I am a gifted and anointed author. I write, publish, and sell books that transform people's lives.

Today, I choose to agree with God! I proclaim today will be a good day. I will complete the tasks before me. I will work diligently with what has been placed in my care.

Today, I choose to agree with God! This is the day for me to proclaim that sales and commissions are coming to me.

Today, I choose to agree with God! I honor God with the work of my hands. I honor Him with the fruit of my labor. As a result, I am blessed in all areas of my life.

Today, I choose to agree with God! I meditate on God's Word day and night. I believe what His Word says about me. I am designed to live a successful, abundant, and prosperous life.

Today, I choose to agree with God! I have the creative power of God on the inside of me. I am blessed and able to achieve anything I desire.

Today, I choose to agree with God! I proclaim today is a get-it-done kind of day. I will move forward those projects I have been procrastinating or avoiding. No more delay for me today!

Today, I choose to agree with God! I am a runner, and I run to win.

19

Kingdom Influence

"You are the salt of the earth; but if the salt loses its flavor, how shall it be seasoned? It is then good for nothing but to be thrown out and trampled underfoot by men. You are the light of the world. A city that is set on a hill cannot be hidden. Nor do they light a lamp and put it under a basket, but on a lampstand, and it gives light to all who are in the house. Let your light so shine before men, that they may see your good works and glorify your Father in heaven" (Matthew 5:13-16 NKJV).

"Give instruction to a wise man, and he will be still wiser; Teach a just man, and he will increase in learning" (Proverbs 9:9 NKJV).

"As iron sharpens iron, So a man sharpens the countenance of his friend" (Proverbs 27:17 NKJV).

PROCLAMATIONS

Today, I choose to agree with God! I am a carrier of the manifested reality of God's goodness. Signs and wonders follow me everywhere I go.

Today, I choose to agree with God! The Kingdom of God is forever increasing in me and through me. Life in the Kingdom is so much fun!

Today, I choose to agree with God! I am bold. I am bold. I am bold. I am the righteousness of God, and the righteous are bold as a lion.

Today, I choose to agree with God! I proclaim today will be a good day. I will spread joy and cheer everywhere I go. People will feel loved when I am in the room.

Today, I choose to agree with God! I proclaim today will be seasoned with the presence of God. Everywhere I go, I carry the fragrance of His love and grace.

Today, I choose to agree with God! When I enter a room, the atmosphere changes because God enters the room with me.

Today, I choose to agree with God! I will share the love of God, and make it my goal, to spread happiness and cheer, wherever I go.

Today, I choose to agree with God! I will be nice and kind to those I meet, with a smile and warm heart, I will greet.

Today, I choose to agree with God! The source of all hope, God Himself, lives on the inside of me. I am a hope-filled person.

Today, I choose to agree with God! I am strong and courageous. I open my mouth and release words of encouragement over people everywhere that I go.

Today, I choose to agree with God! I proclaim that God's presence and love surround me daily. I carry him with me wherever I go.

Today, I choose to agree with God! I am a carrier of the Healer and He is always ready to heal. People are healed everywhere that I go because of His healing presence in me.

Today, I choose to agree with God! I have contagious faith. Whenever someone gets around me it won't be long before they start believing at a whole new level.

Today, I choose to agree with God! The Word of God is living and moving. Jesus is the Word and He is living and moving in and through me!

Today, I choose to agree with God! I heal the sick, raise the dead, and cast out devils.

Today, I choose to agree with God! I have been given power and authority. I am an extension cord to the power and authority of God.

Today, I choose to agree with God! I see people through the eyes of God. I see each and every person, not according to their current state, but according to their full potential.

20

Power Behind Your Words

As a child of God, you have the power and ability to direct and influence the course of events.

"The Spirit of the Lord is upon Me, Because He has anointed Me To preach the gospel to the poor; He has sent Me to heal the brokenhearted,

To proclaim liberty to the captives And recovery of sight to the blind, To set at liberty those who are oppressed" (Luke 4:18 NKJV).

"Pleasant words are like a honeycomb, Sweetness to the soul and health to the bones" (Proverbs 16:24).

"Let no corrupt word proceed out of your mouth, but what is good for necessary edification, that it may impart grace to the hearers" (Ephesians 4:29).

"Death and life are in the power of the tongue, And those who love it will eat its fruit" (Proverbs 18:21 NKJV).

PROCLAMATIONS

Today, I choose to agree with God! I speak pleasant words that are sweet to the soul and healing to the bones. I am wise, and I bring healing.

Today, I choose to agree with God! I will speak life to my future. God has great plans for me and my best and most blessed days are in front of me, not behind me.

Today, I choose to agree with God! I speak words of life over myself, my loved ones, my family, and my friends. I am satisfied by the good produced with the fruit of my lips.

Today, I choose to agree with God! I will speak words of faith, hope, and love. The Lord has put a watch over the words of my mouth, and He guards the fruit of my lips to keep me from stumbling.

Today, I choose to agree with God! My words are powerful and my heart overflows with life. When I speak, life comes out of my mouth.

Today, I choose to agree with God! I speak words that impart grace to the one that I am speaking to. That person is then able to do something they previously were not able to do.

Today, I choose to agree with God! I declare that my words have power. When I pray, heaven hears. My prayers are powerful and effective.

Today, I choose to agree with God! I speak God's Word, and it does not return void. His Word accomplishes what He pleases, and it prospers in the thing for which it is sent.

Today, I choose to agree with God! A good word can bring healing. I have the good Word on my lips. People are healed when I speak.

As I lay my worries
and burdens at His
feet, He promises to
give me rest.

21

Promises

G od has declared and given His promise (Word)
as assurances that He will do what He has proclaimed.

"For all the promises of God in Him are Yes, and
in Him Amen, to the glory of God through us" (2
Corinthians 1:20 NKJV).

"Fear not, for I am with you; Be not dismayed, for I
am your God. I will strengthen you, Yes, I will help
you, I will uphold you with My righteous right hand"
(Isaiah 41:10).

"For the mountains shall depart And the hills be
removed, But My kindness shall not depart from
you, Nor shall My covenant of peace be removed,"
Says the LORD, who has mercy on you (Isaiah 54:10
NKJV).

PROCLAMATIONS

Today, I choose to agree with God! He started a really good thing in me, and He will see it through to the end!

Today, I choose to agree with God! I'm walking on the water of the Word. I stand on God's promises. I believe what I have heard.

Today, I choose to agree with God! As I commit my work to the Lord, He will establish my plans and it will go well with me.

Today, I choose to agree with God! As I lay my worries and burdens at His feet, He promises to give me rest.

22

Wealth and Prosperity

The promise of God to His family is that He is able to make all grace abound toward you and that you will always, in everything, prosper and abound in every good work.

"And the Lord will grant you plenty of goods, in the fruit of your body, in the increase of your livestock, and in the produce of your ground, in the land of which the Lord swore to your fathers to give you. The Lord will open to you His good treasure, the heavens, to give the rain to your land in its season, and to bless all the work of your hand. You shall lend to many nations, but you shall not borrow" (Deuteronomy 28:11-12 NKJV).

"And God is able to make all grace abound toward you, that you, always having all sufficiency in all things, may have an abundance for every good work" (2 Corinthians 9:8).

PROCLAMATIONS

Today, I choose to agree with God! God delights in my desires and my prosperity.

Today, I choose to agree with God! God provides for all of my needs. I have no lack in my life. God abundantly blesses me. The work of my hands prospers daily.

Today, I choose to agree with God! I proclaim that I am blessed and not cursed. God has empowered me to live as a champion. Everything I put my hand to prospers.

Today, I choose to agree with God! I give again and again, and I am made very rich and wealthy. I am always watering and refreshing others, and I am watered and refreshed, too!

Today, I choose to agree with God! I proclaim that I am the head, and not the tail. I am above and not beneath. God has given me the ability to get wealth.

Today, I choose to agree with God! I will walk in abundance and prosperity. I have the ability to create a happy and joyful life. Today, I will make the most of my time and resources.

Today, I choose to agree with God! I am a financier of the Kingdom of God. I call in resources from the north, south, east, and west. Money comes to me quickly and easily.

Today, I choose to agree with God! I am called to be in charge of great sums of money. I am a generous giver. I enjoy blessing others with my wealth.

Today, I choose to agree with God! God has given me the power and ability to get wealth. I refuse to be poor. I embrace the riches that God has set aside for me.

Today, I choose to agree with God! God blesses me with benefits daily. He is my source and my provider. God takes pleasure in my prosperity because He loves me greatly.

Today, I choose to agree with God! I have ideas that make money, and I know how to invest that money to make even more. I am prosperous for kingdom purposes.

Today, I choose to agree with God! Money flows freely each and every day. It flows to me directly, and listens to what I say.

Today, I choose to agree with God! My money is blessed. I speak to my money, I tell it to stay, my finances flow, from the Great Yahweh!

Today, I choose to agree with God! I am awakened to the reality that prosperity is a part of my salvation experience.

Today, I choose to agree with God! I am a money magnet. I delight in the Word day and night and everything I do prospers.

23

Be A Voice

And the Word became flesh and dwelt among us, and we beheld His glory, the glory as of the only begotten of the Father, full of grace and truth. – John 1:14

Jesus is the Word, that is, the voice of God made flesh and the redeemed are the flesh becoming the Word, the voice, to all the earth. The Lord has a voice, and He is always transmitting. He speaks into the earthly realm in many ways:

1. The heavens declare His glory and the earth His handiwork (Psalm 19:1)

2. Through His prophets (Hosea 1:10; Hebrews 1:1)

3. Through the Holy Spirit (John 16:13; Acts 16:6)

4. Through Scripture (Hebrews 4:12)

5. Through Jesus (John 14:9)

6. Through His church

The Purpose of God's Voice:

God's voice comes to:

1. Communicate

2. Articulate

3. Declare

4. State

5. Assert

6. Reveal

7. Proclaim

8. Announce

We have talked about the power that the Word of God carries, and being sensitive to praying the Word of God rather than the problem. We know now that the things of God become ours by the reason of use, and we know the importance of aligning ourselves with God's Word. From shifting our circumstances into a position of favor, to partnering our words with our faith and hearing God's voice, every situation carries the potential for change depending on the words spoken into and over it. If we consider how the promises of God have, and will continue, to affect each of us as individuals, how God's Word reverberates in families, communities, neighborhoods, and economies, why could we not think that we, corporately, have the power to change entire governments and nations?

"Blessed is the nation whose God is the LORD, The people He has chosen as His own inheritance" (Psalm 33:12).

The Bible instructs us to pray for the affairs of our government and nations. In this ungodly world, we must stand up for righteousness and fight a good fight.

"The effective, fervent prayer of a righteous man avails much. Elijah was a man with a nature like ours, and he prayed earnestly that it would not rain; and it did not rain on the land for three years and six months. And he prayed again, and the heaven gave rain, and the earth produced its fruit" (James 5:16-18).

Therefore, I exhort first of all that supplications, prayers, intercessions, and giving of thanks be made for all men, for kings and all who are in authority, that we may lead a quiet and peaceable life in all godliness and reverence. For this is good and acceptable in the sight of God our Savior . . . (1 Timothy 2:1-3 NKJV).

Life and death are in the words we choose to speak. God's Word is spirit and life and has the power to perform itself. We can be a life-changing voice in the earth, and with the governments of the earth, as we choose to agree with God's Word and make the following proclamations:

PROCLAMATIONS

Today, I choose to agree with God! I will pray, intercede, and give thanks for all who are in positions of authority that they lead quiet and peaceable lives in all godliness and reverence.

Today, I choose to agree with God! I proclaim that my government leaders and those in positions of authority are focused, turn aside from idle talk, and have a heart's desire to teach from the platform of their positions.

Today, I choose to agree with God! I proclaim that my government leaders and those in positions of authority have a firm understanding of the things they say, and the things which they affirm.

Today, I choose to agree with God! I proclaim that our leaders and those in positions of authority are the husbands of one wife, and that all are temperate, sober-minded, of good behavior, dress and act with propriety, and in moderation.

Today, I choose to agree with God! I proclaim that our leaders and those in positions of authority are hospitable, not given to excessive alcohol or harmful substance activities, do not engage in violent or abusive behaviors toward others, and are respectful toward all people.

Today, I choose to agree with God! I proclaim that our leaders and those in positions of authority will not be greedy for money, will not be covetous, will be gentle, and not quarrelsome.

Today, I choose to agree with God! I proclaim that our leaders and those in positions of authority will be ones who rule their own houses well having their children in submission with all reverence.

Today, I choose to agree with God! I proclaim that our leaders and those in positions of authority who rule well will be counted worthy of double honor.

Today, I choose to agree with God! I proclaim that our leaders and those in positions of authority will not be novices, puffed up with pride, but will have a good testimony for those in their path.

Today, I choose to agree with God! I proclaim that our leaders and those in positions of authority will not be double-tongued, and will have first been tested and found blameless before assuming their positions.

Today, I choose to agree with God! I proclaim that our leaders and those in positions of authority will be an example to others in word, conduct, love, spirit, faith, and purity.

Today, I choose to agree with God! I proclaim that our leaders and those in positions of authority are rich in good works, always ready to give, and willing to share.

Today, I choose to agree with God! I proclaim that our leaders and those in positions of authority will speak words that are wholesome, and refrain from disputes, arguments, envy, and strife.

Today, I choose to agree with God! I proclaim that our leaders and those in positions of authority will be teachers in faith, and truth.

If My people who are called by My name will humble themselves, and pray and seek My face, and turn from their wicked ways, then I will hear from heaven, and will forgive their sin and heal their land (2 Chronicles 7:14 NKJV).

PRAYER FOR THE GOVERNMENT

Father, in Jesus' name, we pray for our country and its government. We bring before You in prayer the men and women who are in positions of leadership and authority. We pray and intercede for the president, representatives of all levels of our government, and all those who are in authority over us in any way. We pray that the Spirit of the Lord rests upon them. We pray that skillful and godly wisdom will enter into the heart of our president and government representatives. Discretion watches over them, understanding keeps them, and delivers them from the way of evil, and from evil company.

Father, we pray that the leaders of our government are men and women who make their hearts and ears attentive to godly counsel and do that which is right in Your sight. We pray You cause them to be men and women of integrity. We pray that the upright shall dwell in our government. They will be men and women blameless and complete in Your sight. We pray that the wicked shall be cut off from our government, and the treacherous shall be rooted out of it.

It is written in Your Word that the heart of the king is in the hand of the Lord and that You turn it whichever way You desire. We pray that the hearts of our leaders are in Your hand, and that their decisions are divinely directed by You.

We pray that the good news of the gospel is published in our land, and that the Word of the Lord prevails and grows mightily in the hearts and lives of our government officials. We pray for this land and the leaders You have given us, in Jesus' Name. Amen!

About the Author

Dr. Clarice Fluitt is an internationally recognized Christian leader, author, popular television personality, and television host of Wisdom to Win. For more than four decades, she has had a distinguished worldwide reputation as a Christian mentor. Her success is based on her ability to assist ministries, organizations, and individuals achieve real results. Her experiences as a mentor, enterprising businesswoman, and strategic consultant allow her to share her proven strategies for building the Kingdom, inspiring individuals, and generating sustainable growth.

Dr. Fluitt is a time proven prophetess with laser like accuracy. Reports of amazing miracles and healings with positive life changing evidence continually follow her ministry. Dr. Clarice's life is a remarkable chronicle of hilarious real-life stories, tragic trials, tests, and moving visitations of the Lord. Unpretentious and friendly, she is a highly-esteemed minister and conference speaker.

Drawing from her background in marketplace and Christian ministry, national and international church and mentoring school training and development, leadership expertise, and world-wide speaking engagements, Dr. Fluitt touches lives through her wisdom, wit, and extraordinary insight, providing avenues of transformational change to individuals from every walk of life.

More Resources by Dr. Clarice Fluitt

Books

Ridiculous Miracles

The Law of Honor

Inspirational Insights

Thoughts That Make You Think

Developing Your Limitless Potential

Living the Unhindered Life

Think Like a Champion and Win

Experiencing the Power of God's Word

Contact Information

Clarice Fluitt Enterprises, LLC

P O Box 15111 Monroe, LA 71207

Website

www.claricefluitt.com

www.claricefluitt.org